THE **ACCIDENTAL**
ENTREPRENEUR

How I Stumbled into Success

FREDERICK BRODSKY

TO DARLA CHICK BRODSKY,

my partner in the great adventure of life.

CONTENTS

1

GOING NOWHERE FAST

I BELIEVE THAT EVERYTHING HAS A SOUL.
If you think of a soul as energy, then it's easy to say that every living thing has a soul. Plants have been known to respond to music and conversation. That type of thinking makes it difficult for me to do any kind of landscaping because I'll always try to nurse the sickest plants back to health. I'd go so far as to say a piece of art has a soul to some extent because art clearly possesses energy, even if we aren't able to comprehend that as human beings. Animals clearly have souls, and when you watch an interaction between a person and an animal, it becomes evident that we're not smart enough to communicate everything.

I've experienced a connection with a lot of different animals over the years, including dogs, cats, a white rat, and even a lion. Growing up in Woodbridge, New Jersey, in the 1940s, we lived in a house at the end of a tiny dirt road. The house may have been small, but it was always filled with animals for as long as I could remember. And not just dogs, but ducks and chickens. One summer, I came back from camp with a white rat who I creatively named Whitey. After settling into our home, Whitey gnawed his way out of his cage. I tore apart the house looking for him, only to find him later that night curled up in my bed, fast asleep. I also remember sitting on the steps to the basement feeding our baby goat with a bottle. And at one point, we had fifty parakeets. Fifty. We started with just one. His name was Danny Boy, and he had the run of the house. When my dad would come back from the bakery he owned, Danny Boy would climb up on his chest, and they would fall asleep together.

I have no idea where all of our animals came from, but it was most likely my dad's influence. He was the animal lover. My mother tolerated the animals, but she did end up liking Whitey the rat. She wanted nothing to do with him at first but grew so comfortable that he would climb up on her shoulder when she was cooking in the kitchen. When my parents had friends over, I delighted in putting Whitey up my sleeve and then watching their reaction when he stuck his pink nose out as I went to shake their hands. That would scare the hell out of our guests!

My father and I might have shared a love for animals, but it was my mother who ended up having the most significant impact on me. It was her lifestyle and worldview that I learned to appreciate as I got older. She came from a wealthy family in Odessa, which was a part of Russia at the time, and was educated at Cambridge in China before settling in the United States. She was a pretty woman, so vivacious and cosmopolitan that she attracted an eclectic group of friends. As I grew older, my mother's style of living and worldly nature began to rub off on me. And since she was also stubborn and used to getting her way, I have no doubt that is what influenced my independence.

My father couldn't have been more different. He had no formal education, but he was knowledgeable about many things and had incredible street smarts. He literally walked from Odessa to France as a young man to avoid joining the Russian army. He survived the trip and made it to the United States, where he later joined his family in Brooklyn. When I was a kid, he converted our original garage into a master bedroom, complete with a sunroom. He built a den in the front of the house and an entirely new garage and workshop in the backyard. He did it all by himself and it lasted—there were never any leaks or structural problems. He was very much a rough and rugged guy who was not sophisticated at all, but he was curious, so he asked great questions. He also dressed well, was a lot of fun and a great dancer. I wouldn't believe it if I didn't see it for myself, but there is a video of him gracefully dancing with my mother at my Bar Mitzvah.

My parents met back in 1938 and married out of necessity—my mom was twenty-seven and not yet married. My father was an older, good-looking man of thirty-nine who came from a large family in New York, so he was an attractive marriage prospect. He then became part-owner in a bakery, and that was how he supported the family. Both my parents worked at the bakery, so my mom hired our neighbor Matilda Toth from across the road to cook, clean the house, and look after me and my younger brother, Greg.

I was a difficult child from the get-go. I was never in trouble with the law or anything like that, but I didn't listen. When I would do something wrong, my mom used to say, "You're a snot-nosed kid. You don't have a pot to piss in. Who do you think you are?" Sometimes my parents would get so frustrated that they would threaten to leave me alone. I only got them more upset when I'd respond by saying, "How much food is in the refrigerator?" While I respected my mother and wanted to please her, she did not intimidate me, and her threats had little impact on my actions. Most of my decisions were my own.

My parents thought I was a pain in the ass, but they doted on my brother, Greg, who was two years younger. I heard a story that after I was born, my mom used to cover my face and tell people I was sleeping because she didn't think I was a very attractive child. But when Greg came along, he could do no wrong in my parents' eyes. They enrolled him at Admiral Farragut Academy in Toms River, New Jersey, which was a prep school for the Naval Academy, while I stayed home and went to public school in Woodbridge. Even when he was older, he was always trotted out and patted on the head. With me, it was the opposite.

When I really did something wrong, my dad would discipline me with his belt. He was a baker, so he wore white pants and had this wide, black, leather belt. And he would hit hard. One summer, I broke something in the house. I knew what was coming, so I bolted for the front door before he could get his belt off. I was running so fast that I went right through the screen door. I didn't return home until dark, but he was waiting up for me and beat the hell out of me with that belt when I walked inside.

By the time I was eleven, my parents had enough, so they shipped me off to live with my grandparents in Florida. The only person who could handle my mother was my grandmother, Celia, so the logic was that she could bring me around, too. You wouldn't know it to look at her, but my grandmother was four feet and eleven inches of absolute steel. I may have towered over her, but she wouldn't hesitate to smack me in the chest when I did something wrong. All I could do was stand there and take it. I wasn't in Florida long before I learned to respect her.

My grandmother may have ruled with an iron fist, but my grandfather was the complete opposite. His name was Elkan Flaum, and he wasn't my grandfather by blood—my maternal grandfather had been killed in the Russian Revolution, so my grandmother had been married twice—but he was a genuinely gentle person even though he was a big man who must have been six feet two or six feet three. It was quite the sight to watch my grandmother dominate my grandfather with her will and character, but he was so calm and mellow that he could take it all in stride without being a pushover. I admired the way he could absorb her volatility and then carry on his way without ever letting it affect him. It was like he was off on his own island in the middle of a violent sea.

I loved spending time with my grandfather. He used to take me fishing off the bridges between the islands by Miami Beach. Sometimes we'd go on day charters and join forty other guys fishing off the side of the boat. He loved to fish, but he would also take me to ride horses and ponies on the weekend, and I got pretty good at riding during my time there.

I stayed in Florida for a year, which meant that I had to enroll in school. I was ahead of the kids since I had already learned most of the curriculum back in New Jersey, so school came pretty easy. I made some friends, and I'd even take the bus by myself down to Miami Beach. My grandparents gave me the freedom to venture off on my own and enjoy many experiences, like buying six White Castle hamburgers for one dollar. That year in Florida may have straightened me out a little, but when I returned to Woodbridge, it was more of the same. I continued to find new ways to disappoint my parents.

Every year, a group of five kids were chosen to take the role of the adults for one day in the Jewish Community Center at our synagogue in Woodbridge. I was elected president and asked to say something about the Jewish community after services on Friday night. I don't know if there had been more talking during service that night than usual, but I chose to speak my mind and call out the blatant hypocrisy I'd witnessed all around me. People would come into services late, others would talk right through it, and some would even sleep. That ticked me off because I actually enjoyed the services for the most part; it wasn't a chore for me. It also bothered me to watch some of the leaders of the community come into service wearing their new furs and jewels. So many people seemed more concerned with what everyone was wearing than they were with the service itself, so that's what I chose to call out during my speech. The leaders didn't like that, and my parents especially didn't like my comments. My mother had a fit. Once again, I was an embarrassment.

I was a loner when I was a kid. I had friends, so I wasn't antisocial, but I always liked animals more than I did people, which was probably why I spent so much time alone. Out of all of our animals we had over the years, I was closest to our collie, Skippy. We were at a farmer's market auction being held outside of Woodbridge when I saw him shivering under a table and convinced my parents to buy him. I used to lie in the grass and play with him. Sometimes, we'd hang out in the underground fort I had built in the large, five-acre field across the road from our house. It was about five feet deep, six-by-six, and covered with boards and sod on top, so you couldn't see it unless you were really looking for it—just one of the benefits of growing up in the house at the far end of the road with fields to the south and west. At least when I was home and by myself, I wasn't able to get into as much trouble.

I may have been a difficult child, but I was a good student, and I always worked hard. Soon after I returned from Florida, I went to work for Charlie Kaufman. He was a friend of my parents who owned a flannel pajama factory. I don't remember if it was my idea or my parents' idea, but I didn't mind working. My allowance was small, and I wanted more spending money. That was the first time I had to punch a clock to earn an hourly wage, and I earned every penny. I had to carry the cut flannel up and down four flights of stairs during my shift. It was grueling, but that job really built up my legs.

Over the summer when Greg went to camp at Admiral Farragut Academy in New Jersey, I worked there as the head waiter. During my time off, I learned how to sail. The boat was a twelve-foot Barnegat Bay sneakbox made out of wood. It had a little jib and a gaff rig, and was a robust little boat that was a lot of fun to sail. Sailing was peaceful and relaxing, but what I really enjoyed was being out there on my own. It was up to me to make the boat perform. It was a challenge—an individual challenge—and for someone very comfortable being independent, that appealed to me. They also let us go out on rides in an old PT boat from the Second World War. It had been retired ten years earlier, but they would rev it up and take us around Toms River. That was my first exposure to boating, and I loved it!

Every once in a while, I managed to make my parents proud, and never did I make them prouder than I did during my Bar Mitzvah when I was thirteen. I know my dad was especially proud when I read the Torah and gave my speech during the Friday night ceremony. I was becoming a man, and it was a big deal for my father, who was autocratic and proud. Coming from Russia, he was conservative, leaning toward orthodox.

My dad and I didn't talk much. He didn't know anything about what men in America often talk about, which is sports. Instead, he spent most of his time working, and he worked very hard. He would get up at 3:00 a.m., so he could get to the bakery by 4:00 a.m. He'd come home around noon, have lunch, and then take a nap for a couple of hours. I'd go to bed soon after dinner, around 8:00 p.m., so we didn't cross paths often. Every once in a while, we'd drive into New York, or take the Staten Island ferry to meet his family in Brooklyn. We didn't do that too often, but it was interesting to meet my cousins, and his brother and sister, Benny and Betty, because their lifestyle was more orthodox and quite different from ours. The only real time I got to share with my father was when I went with him to work in the bakery. I really enjoyed being there during the holidays, and when I was old enough to use the bread slicing machines, I could help out more.

I was still thirteen and at summer camp with Greg when we learned that our dad had died. He was fifty-four years old and had suffered his fourth heart attack. Matilda drove down to pick us up and bring us home. Some of my mom's well-intentioned friends would approach me and say things like, "You have to be the man of the house now," and, "It's up to you to look after your mom." I'd never had those father-son conversations like a lot of kids do with their dads, and I didn't have a deep bond with my father, so I never experienced any great sense of loss, but my brother took the news hard. I believe Greg felt slighted because our father died before his Bar Mitzvah, so he never had the same experience with him that I did. I'm not sure Greg ever recovered from that.

I may not have been close to my father, but I like to think I inherited some of his common sense, logic, and curiosity. After the funeral, I sat at the end of my bed and couldn't help but feel very much alone. I told myself that it was up to me to make happen what I wanted to happen. Having been independent for most of my life, it didn't feel like that far of a reach, so I carried on. Meanwhile, my mother became more involved in the bakery, and when I became old enough to drive, I'd drive the bakery truck and help out with the deliveries.

I was able to save my money over the years because I never bought frivolous things—fashion never appealed to me and it still does not. I'd go to movies, buy model airplanes, and spend money on dates, but not much. Dates would cost me $2. My first real girlfriend was Donna Lee Carroll. Her parents were strict Catholics and were not happy that their daughter was dating a Jewish guy, but I had great affection for her and still do. We dated junior and senior years and went to the prom together senior year.

My big purchase was a car. As a kid, I got around by bus (round-trip bus fare to Perth Amboy was $0.50, and $1 when I had a date), but by seventeen, I had saved up enough to buy a black Ford Fairlane convertible with a spare tire continental kit and red leather interior for $1,300—and I paid in cash. But just because I had a car didn't mean that I was going to stop working. When I graduated high school in 1958, I got a job that summer as a deck boy at a casino in Long Branch, New Jersey. They played cards there, but it wasn't a gambling casino—more like a swimming pool club on the beach. My job was to wait on the card players at the tables and those lounging around the pool. I'd get them sandwiches, drinks, decks of cards, and string the tables to prevent the cards from being blown away when it was windy. That job was how I gained fascinating insights into who was comfortable with their money and who wasn't.

One breezy afternoon, two couples were playing cards at a table outside—one couple was old money and the other couple was newly wealthy. It immediately became clear to me that the new money couple felt the need to impress, as they kept demanding drinks and service without considering that all the other tables were full, and I was incredibly busy. At one point, the man snapped his fingers to get my attention, which garnered a look of disdain from the old money couple. When it came time to settle the bill after three hours, the old money couple left a generous tip while the new money couple left a pittance. Even though both couples frequented the club, I never saw them playing cards together again.

That summer, my mother had begun to socialize more, so she was always out of the house and left my brother and me alone, but the two of us were never that close. He didn't have the same attitude I did toward animals or living things. We had completely different value systems, so we fought a lot and kept our distance from each other.

I may have been independent, but I didn't avoid people or groups either. I played basketball down in Long Branch, and made friends through the Jewish community, but I continued to keep to myself as I got older. And when left to yourself, you have time to think.

The world had changed a lot during the 1950s. Space exploration was in its embryonic stage, and that led me to think more about our universe. Was space infinite? Were we alone? I don't know if it was my concept of spirituality, or the way I believed that the universe was comprised of 100 percent energy (when something lost energy, something else gained energy), but I never believed we were alone. I still don't.

I was equally fascinated by the shuttles and the equipment that were testing the limits of our atmosphere at that time. I'd go up to the attic of our house and tack up pictures of the Bell X-1, which was the first airplane to break the sound barrier. I put up maps of the stars and the constellations. The more I read about things like the singularity concept and all the studies being done on the planets, the more I became interested in space, so I enrolled at Rutgers University as a science major because I wanted to become an astrophysicist.

For all my interest in space and exploring the unknown, it turned out that I had little interest in the other sciences. Chemistry, physics, calculus, analytical geometry, and German were the classes I had to take; I wasn't studying space at all. I didn't appreciate what went into becoming an astrophysicist, so I became more interested in the sailing club and partying with a young woman who also happened to be Miss Apple Blossom of New Jersey. She became my preoccupation that first semester. Meanwhile, in the classroom, I succeeded in failing five of my seven subjects, so I switched to pre-law before my second semester.

My grades improved significantly, but halfway through my second semester, I received a letter, informing me that I had been kicked out of school due to my poor first semester grades. One of my professors tried to appeal to the administration, saying that I was a good student and was doing well, but it was a futile effort. I was extremely disappointed and thought it was unfair, but the administration decided that I was too immature despite my recent progress. They wanted me to take the time to grow up before returning to school. One night, they did find me passed out in my dorm elevator, so they had a point.

Unfortunately, my mother got the same letter I did. I honestly don't remember her reaction. I must have blocked it out of my brain, but I can say for certain that she was disappointed and did everything in her power to save face. My mother was very social and had a lot of powerful friends, one of whom was the Secretary of State of New Jersey, who she asked to call in a favor with Rutgers, the state university, but there was nothing anyone could do.

I moved back home, and in our small Jewish community of two hundred families, I was an outcast and a complete embarrassment to my mother, who sent me to work for a friend of hers at an industrial warehouse that supplied construction materials to building sites. I drove the delivery truck and used the forklift to stack pallets in the warehouse. It sounded simple enough, but the local Teamsters became very upset with me because I was one of the few non-union workers at the warehouse. They had some very direct conversations with me about joining, but that never appealed to me, and neither did moving fifty-pound cement bags from one freight car to another, so I didn't stay there very long.

Instead of trying to pick up the pieces or come up with a plan to return to college, I decided to go in a different direction. I took a job as a toll collector at the New Jersey Turnpike. It was easy, and there were enough people passing through every day to keep it interesting. One of the perks was that the girls driving through on their way to the Jersey Shore would invite my friend Johnny Tatola and me to parties. Johnny and I would work all day, party all night, and then sleep on the beach before getting up and doing it all over again the next day. I was coming out of my shell. I dated quite a bit after high school, and that quickly cured me of any remaining shyness from my youth.

It's unfair to say that I completely lacked direction or ambition because I did have ideas, misguided as they may have been. While playing basketball in Long Branch, I met a group of guys in a rock band called The Satellites, who used to play at local parties. I came up with the foolproof idea of managing the group. We made two demo records of their own songs, and I took them with me up to New York to try to get them a record contract. I wasn't able to get the deal, though we did land a spot during amateur night at the Apollo Theater in Harlem. When our lead singer froze on stage, they hauled him off with a crook, one of those hooks used to herd sheep. The group performed a couple of more times down at the Jersey Shore, but that was about it. My career as the manager of a rock and roll group never quite panned out.

I enjoyed my hedonistic lifestyle, but after about a year, my mom had enough of my attitude and my complete lack of direction or concern for my own future, so she came up with a new plan, and it was drastic. Not only would her plan take me out of New Jersey. It would take me out of the country.

2

THE UGLY AMERICAN

S **HORTLY AFTER THE RUSSIAN REVOLUTION** in March 1917, my grandfather left the family home in Samara, Russia, one night to attend an important political meeting. His coachman drove him away, and my grandfather was never seen again.

After my grandfather's apparent murder, and given his leftist political leanings, and that he was in favor of deposing the Tsar, my grandmother knew that the remaining family would be targeted. So, in early 1918, she packed up what she could carry and, with the help of the servants, buried the other valuables on the property. She then fled their beautiful home with her five-year-old daughter (who would become my mother) and her seven-year-old son, Walter, aboard the Trans-Siberian Railway headed for China. This was my four-foot-eleven grandmother traveling alone with two young children. That required fortitude, and she had to learn how to be resourceful. Before leaving, she put her jewels in the lining of her coat to bribe officials and help pay for train tickets.

After three weeks, they stopped in Yakutsk, Russia, which happened to be the second coldest large city in the world. While my grandmother stayed home with my mother, Walter learned how to trade and sell in the open-air bazaar. He started with handkerchiefs and expanded to include napkins, pillowcases, and tablecloths, but it wasn't enough. The harsh winter and their dwindling resources forced my grandmother to send now nine-year-old Walter back to Russia alone to retrieve the valuables that had been buried on the property. Since he was enrolled in the musical institute, he could obtain a travel order by claiming to be picking up sheet music, which was in short supply. The trip home took three weeks, but upon his return to Samara, the buried valuables were nowhere to be found. Luckily, his aunt gave him some money—she sewed ten gold coins into his boots for the three-week journey back. The bulk of the valuables were never recovered, but the diamond ring my grandmother traveled with was passed down to my mom, who then gave it to me to use as an engagement ring for my wife, Darla, so it remains in the family to this day.

Upon Walter's return to Yakutsk, my grandmother immediately started planning their departure. The small family was on the road for an entire year as they traveled across Russia and into Manchuria and Mongolia, where my grandmother acquired protection from a chieftain by becoming one of his concubines—a drastic change from the comfortable lifestyle to which the family had grown accustomed back in Russia. My grandmother later convinced the chieftain to help her complete the family's journey to Harbin, China, where she would reunite with my uncle. Once settled in Harbin, my grandmother worked as a seamstress, while my mother attended school in a convent, and Walter hustled on the street.

As Walter grew older, he never lost his adventurous spirit. When nineteen, he was sent to Mongolia to buy a load of fur. It was his first real job. Back then, everyone traveled by horseback, so the journeys were long. After finally arriving, he wanted to pack up his load and leave, but the chieftain insisted he stay as their guest. Walter was invited to a big feast in his honor where he was fed all kinds of food and liquor. That night, three young ladies kept him warm and comfortable. In the morning, a very hungover Walter weighed all of the furs (furs were sold by weight back then), paid for the goods, loaded the furs on to the packhorses, and set out on the ten-day trip south. By the time he arrived at his destination to sell the load, it was thirty kilos lighter than it was when he had first weighed it. What had happened was that the chieftain and his people wet the furs, so they froze at night and were heavier when weighed the next morning. Over the journey, the ice melted, the water drained, and the furs dried out, thus making them lighter and worth less money than Walter had paid. He got burned, but he learned his first lesson in business—if something seems too good to be true, take a closer look. He took that lesson to heart and turned into quite the astute trader.

Walter worked constantly and built up his own business. He soon became a world-renowned expert in bristles for hair and shaving brushes. With Paul Donnay, he was co-owner of the Chanel franchise in Hong Kong. He also owned a sausage-casing factory in Germany, but most of his business was in selling fur and animal products. He was the largest buyer of furs at the Canton Trade Fair in China for the English fur market, one of his major client bases.

It wasn't just his professional success that set him apart; my uncle was a fascinating character. He was serious, quiet, but was also charming, self-assured, and very large and imposing. He must have been six feet two and 250 pounds, and he remained athletic until his later years. He played soccer and raced sulkies (one-horse carriages) while maintaining horse stables in France and Spain. I wouldn't call him intimidating; it was more that he was impressive. Walter was a real Renaissance man who could not only speak eight languages, but he could read and write in those languages as well, and he loved to read all kinds of books.

I had only met him briefly as a child when he came to visit our family—once in New Jersey and once in Canada. We didn't spend much time together, but I could immediately understand why my mother looked up to him. He was gracious, and although he was relatively quiet, he would always be the life of the party when he entertained. And he was a ladies' man for sure.

By 1959, Walter was forty-nine years old and an extremely successful business owner. Universal Animal Products (UAP) was the name of his company, and his main office was located in Paris. That's where my mother decided to send her nineteen-year-old son. I was hesitant to go at first because I was being deprived of my independence, but there was no wiggle room—she was kicking me out of the house, and I had no say in the matter. She made sure to tell me, "You're going to do whatever he asks you to do. And you better behave yourself!"

It was freezing cold when I boarded the TWA Constellation flight from LaGuardia to Paris. I couldn't read any of the signs on the plane because they were all in French, and I couldn't speak a single word of it either. But I put that out of my mind. At that stage in my life, I didn't think about too many things at all. I was living in the moment. I knew that I was going to work for my uncle, and that was about it.

I can't say for sure how Walter felt about me coming to live with him. When I got off the plane and made it through customs and immigration, I spotted him waiting for me. All he said was "hi." I got the impression that he was reluctant to have me there. It wasn't a warm and fuzzy welcome, but other things were going on with him that day. I was already tired from the trip, so we didn't say much as we walked over to his beautiful, white Mercedes 230 convertible.

We left Paris and drove toward his estate located on Avenue du Général-Leclerc, just opposite the Bois de Saint-Cloud on the outskirts of Paris on the road to Versailles. About twenty minutes into the ride, he told me that he wasn't feeling well. I could tell that he was in pain, and he had grown progressively worse by the time we passed under the enormous wrought iron gates that served as the entrance to his estate. Once inside, he called an ambulance to come take him to the clinic that was about a mile down the road. And just like that, I was by myself in a strange home in a strange country. There were two servants in the estate—a cook who spoke Chinese and French, and a maid who spoke Chinese. Coming from a tiny bungalow in New Jersey, it was overwhelming. I was exhausted from all that had happened, so I took my one small suitcase with me up to the bedroom and did my best to settle in.

When I woke up the next morning, I set out to look for the clinic, but being in a strange city and not speaking the language, it proved to be a difficult task. When I finally arrived, I learned that Walter had passed a kidney stone and would remain in the hospital for the rest of the week. His wife, Galia (I think she was wife number three), arrived later that day. She spoke very little English, so our communication was limited, and she wasn't very talkative. She tended to spend a lot of time away from Paris, but once back at the house, we kept our distance from each other.

The first twenty-four hours may have been surreal, but the first week proved to be relatively uneventful. I did very little but roam around the large house and play with their dog, Bucky. Bucky was a huge boxer, about one hundred pounds, and trained to be a border guard dog in Israel. He was a great companion, and we spent lots of time together walking opposite Walter's estate in the Bois de Saint-Cloud, and, later in my stay, up and down the Champs-Élysées in Paris. A couple of times a day, I would walk up to the clinic to see Walter, but other than that, I didn't do much of anything. I existed, which was a far cry from my active social life back in New Jersey. That all changed when Walter returned home. He immediately put me to work.

Monday morning, we left the estate at 8:00 a.m., and I rode with him to the Paris office, which was on a very small street, Rue Godot-de-Mauroy, and in an area known for being the second most popular spot for prostitutes in the city. Walter rented the third and fourth floors of the office building, but the fourth floor was primarily used to store materials that had been shipped there. There were about six employees in the office, and they were all fairly close. So close that my uncle's go-to man, Heinz, ended up marrying his secretary, Monique.

My first task was to learn about the importing and exporting side of the business by keeping track of commercial purchases, transfers, trades, and sales. What made it difficult was that it was all done in code, a kind of shorthand, because it was expensive to transmit messages back then. I had a codebook to reference and would have to translate each five-letter message to confirm the details of the various transactions.

To avoid getting parking tickets, Walter also wanted me to move his car, which was parked on the street. It sounds simple, but that proved to be quite difficult for me. At the time, Paris had no parking meters and relied on a system called disc parking. This involved putting a small piece of cardboard on the dashboard that had two thumbwheels set up to look like clocks—the first clock for the time the car was parked, and the second for when the car had to be moved. If you tried to cheat by changing either time, you got a parking ticket. I kept forgetting to move Walter's car in time, which resulted in my getting many parking tickets for my uncle.

I did my best to learn French and enrolled in Alliance Française, a language school in Paris, where I studied with an eclectic group of people—all foreigners like me, and all new to France. Some were dancers at the Folies Bergère, a classic show in Paris. Others were waiters, and one was a beautiful Persian girl by the name of Sudi. We were invited a few times to the Folies to see our friends perform, and to restaurants where other students worked, but I couldn't always attend because it wasn't easy for me to get to Paris.

For my transportation, Walter allowed me to drive his Citroen. It was a shift transmission with no separate clutch. You changed gears by flicking a lever at the top of the steering wheel while taking your foot off the gas pedal. It took some time to get used to, along with the hydraulic suspension, but after a while, I got the hang of it.

Slowly, my relationship with my uncle evolved, and after a couple of weeks, he began to warm up to me—at least I think he warmed up to me. Either way, he enjoyed my company enough to invite me out with him. Despite being married, Walter had a very active social life. One of his girlfriends, Henriette, had a younger sister, Eugette, so we used to double date. Henriette could stop traffic—literally. She could whistle so loud that it sounded like a police whistle. Traffic would stop, and she'd lead the way by prancing across the street. The four of us would go out to some very nice restaurants. There was a Chinese restaurant Walter liked called Seventh Floor. Since he spoke Mandarin and Cantonese, and was a generous tipper, the staff would bow and fall all over themselves when we arrived.

After about six weeks, Walter had a new job for me. He owned a textile mill in Aix-en-Provence, which back then was a sleepy town of about forty thousand people in the south of France. The mill cleaned, de-haired, and sorted French cashmere, camel hair, and angora to produce the raw materials that would then be shipped to England. He believed that Andre, the plant manager, was cheating him, and he asked that I be his eyes and ears on the ground. It was an assignment, and one that I felt drastically underqualified to perform, but what choice did I have?

I arrived in Aix-en-Provence via train and stayed at a hotel at first. It wasn't a good hotel. It was more of a little boardinghouse because Walter didn't give me enough money to stay at a nice hotel. The first problem I encountered involved logistics. The factory was three kilometers out of town, and there was no reliable transportation to take me to and from work. I reluctantly had to ask Walter to send me some more money and bought a 125cc Monet Grion motorbike for 120 bucks. I had never ridden a motorbike before, so the salesman gave me a quick tutorial. And I mean quick: "These are the brakes, this is the clutch, and this is the throttle. Here you go!" I got on the bike, zoomed across the street, and immediately crashed.

The salesman helped me back up and said with a strong accent, "You must be English because you were headed for the wrong side of the street."

"I've never ridden a bike before."

"You should have said something. Come here." He climbed onto the bike and motioned for me to get on the back. He had me put my hands on top of his hands, and we spent two hours on the bike driving up the hills and going down these little roads. Pretty soon, I had a feel for the bike, and that's how I learned how to ride.

With my new transportation, I drove to the factory and tried to ask the workers if I could meet with Andre. I received blank stares and suddenly realized that my communication was still limited, despite the French classes back in Paris. However, I did find one worker I could communicate with. Mark was English and in his fifties but had been in France for more than twenty years. He brought me to Andre's office and made the introductions.

Andre was not happy to see me. He wanted nothing to do with me, and I can't blame him for that, but my uncle told him that he wanted me to learn the business, so there I was. Once I got to work, one thing was clear right away—I couldn't have been more underqualified for this job. I had no experience working any of these machines and didn't have a clue what I was doing, but in order for me to take a closer look at the business for my uncle, I first had to learn the operation. I worked Monday through Friday, and with help from Mark, I slowly got the hang of some of the machines. The problem was when the equipment broke down, and it would break down frequently. Fixing those machines and getting the line moving again proved to be quite tricky.

One of my more challenging tasks was blending cashmere and camel hair. It was a job that the other factory workers assigned to me with great glee. In 1959, the blending was done by encasing myself in a coverall with a respirator mask. I'd then take the materials for the blend ratio (such as eighty kilos of camel hair and twenty kilos of cashmere) into a small, windowless room with a high-pressure air hose. I'd then use that hose to try and get as much of the material up in the air at one time as possible, so it would mix together. Each session would take between thirty and forty-five minutes and always left me feeling exhausted.

Andre may have avoided me, but the rest of the workers were great. They showed me the ropes and would joke with me whenever I made a mistake—and there were lots of mistakes, but little by little, I learned how to operate every machine in the plant. It was through working with those guys that I was able to pick up a form of French slang called Argot. Sometimes, Mark would take me out for a beer. At first, we'd talk about the factory and the machines, but the more we talked, the more he opened up to me and eventually shared his story about relocating from England to France.

I was settling in at work, but the hotel was getting expensive, and options were limited. Luckily, I was able to find a much cheaper alternative in the form of a bedroom in a private home. The family allowed me access to the bathroom, but they made it absolutely clear that I was not allowed in the kitchen. I was the only tenant, and since the family spent most of the time in the kitchen, I hardly saw them at all. My rent was dirt cheap, but Aix was not an inexpensive place to live back then, and after eating out at restaurants for a few days in a row, I was running out of money. I had already asked my uncle for money to buy the motorbike, and he was complaining about how much I was spending, so I had to figure something out fast.

I liked to explore. I'd park my bike in town and wander around. Someone had told me there were old Roman public baths down a back alley. When I found them one afternoon, I heard American music coming from this tiny bar across the street. I went inside. The ten-foot-long bar ran along the left wall, and then there were only four or five tables down the right side. Way in the back, there was a little kitchen alcove, and just off to the right, there was the jukebox that kept playing American music. When I saw that kitchen, I got an idea.

The place was empty except for the owner who was behind the bar. His name was Nicki, and he spoke some English, so we started talking. He was from Russia, and I told him how my family came from Russia. Then, I made my pitch. "I don't know anyone here. I work at the textile mill, and I don't make much money. How would you like to make a deal?"

"What kind of deal?"

"You buy the food, and I'll cook it up. You don't even have to pay me." I left out that the extent of my cooking experience involved hot dogs over a campfire.

He thought about it and said, "I usually cook for myself." It sounded like he was going to turn me down at first. "But if you want to cook something, I'll buy the food, and you can cook it for both of us. I'll even let you have some wine, but…" I waited for the catch. "I'll charge you if you drink too much."

That was our arrangement. Sometimes I would go back to my room after work to shower, and sometimes I'd go right to the bar. I cooked a lot of steak, pork, and chicken—all of it panfried. Nicki liked to keep everything simple, so I'd usually cook up a piece of meat and cut it in half for the two of us. Vegetables were slim to none, but I made a salad with oil and vinegar dressing every so often. That was a typical dinner. It wasn't much, but it worked out well for both of us. Nicki was an interesting guy who told some fascinating stories, and over the next couple of weeks, we developed a nice relationship.

I wasn't the only one who was attracted by the American music on the jukebox. There was a base nearby for the French Foreign Legion, and six of the Legionnaires used to come into the bar all the time. They were all good friends, and they could seriously drink. They were from all over Europe, and they were in the bar so often that I got to listen to all of their stories—two of them had been in serious trouble with the law before they joined the Legion. They quickly took a liking to me, and they even looked out for me.

One night, I was sitting at the bar with Nicki when a couple of guys from the local university staggered in. They were loud and obnoxious, and when they learned that I was an American, they started talking to me about American politics. They made it pretty clear that they didn't like Americans, and they didn't like me. They gave me a hard time but left without incident. When I walked out of the bar to go home that night, I saw that the seat of my motorbike had been all cut up. I went back in and told the French Foreign Legion guys, who all came out to take a look. They were really upset. Philippe, who was French and the leader of the group with the biggest motorcycle, said to me, "We'll find them and fix it." I don't know what he did, if anything, but the kids from the university never came back into the bar, and I never had any problem with them again.

The next weekend, the guys in the French Foreign Legion invited me to tag along with them as they made the hour-long trip into Marseilles, which was a pretty rough town back then, but these guys made me feel secure. During the day, we drank and listened to some really great music—flamenco music and music from all over the world.

One night, they took me down a dark alley in Marseilles. I couldn't see a thing. It was pitch black, but we somehow found our way to a door. There was no sign—just a lone, dim lightbulb. One of the guys banged on the door, and a little peephole opened up on the other side, just like you see in the movies. Whoever was back there let us in, and we walked down into this brick-lined cabaret. There was the typical French bar on the left side and tables down the right. At the end, there was this little stage with a guy playing the guitar. He was barely visible because the cigarette smoke was so thick, but I could hear that he was good. We took a seat at one of the tables and were able to catch the last ten minutes of his set. He then thanked the audience in the heaviest Brooklyn accent I had heard in a while. I figured that he had to be from the United States, and it turned out that I was right. When I got up and talked with him, he said he was from Brooklyn and told me a long, convoluted story about how he wound up playing in that bar.

Over the next couple of months, I'd make that trip down to Marseilles a few more times with Philippe and the other Legionnaires. We'd drive along the French coast and stop to party on the beach. They were fascinating people. I could listen to them tell stories for hours. For a country bumpkin who grew up on a dirt road in New Jersey, those discussions and experiences proved to be the start of my cultural education.

When back at the factory, I was finally able to figure out what my uncle had sent me to do. I was lucky because it basically happened by accident. When I walked to the loading dock out back one afternoon, I spotted a pile of materials that were being shipped to England, and then a smaller pile off to the side. I saw one of the guys on the dock and asked, "What is this stuff?"

"That belongs to Andre."

It turned out that Andre would take some of the product and sell it on the side. I had a pretty good idea that's what he had been doing, but it took me a very long time to figure out how he was siphoning it off. I didn't say anything to Andre but told my uncle to compare the weight of the material that was being processed to the weight of material that was being shipped to England. As expected, it was about 15 percent less than it should have been. It would take a little while, but Andre was later fired.

After three months in Aix, my uncle summoned me back to Paris— he even sent me some money for the trip. My room in Aix was week-to-week, so I packed my small bag, bought a pair of cheap goggles, hopped on the motorbike, and set off. Since the motorbike engine was small (only 125cc) I took only back roads and stayed off the major highways. I was on the road for about seven hours before I stopped at a beautiful hotel. I had a lovely dinner and spent the night in a fabulous room where I got a good night's sleep and set out early, first thing in the morning.

Halfway through the day, and still over two hundred miles away from Paris, I reached a small mountain range. Going up the mountain was easy, but on the way down, it started to rain. The conditions were treacherous, and the terrain scared me. There were no guardrails— just a steep drop down the cliff on one side. My cheap goggles kept filling up with water, so I couldn't see anything. I would have to hold the handlebars with one hand while I drained my goggles with the other—alternating hands, so that I could clear each eyepiece. To make matters even worse, the wind was so vicious that I struggled to stay balanced while maneuvering on that tiny two-lane road. Good thing I couldn't see out of my goggles most of the time because I probably would have been more terrified. I gripped the handlebars so tightly that my knuckles turned white for the entire one-hour trip up and down the mountain. It didn't take long for my woolen clothing to get soaked through, and for me to start shaking from the cold.

Once safely back at sea level, I stopped at the nearest bar. I drank two cognacs just to calm down and warm up. It was early afternoon when I set off again through the French countryside, cruising at a top speed of 40 miles per hour. Just when I started to get comfortable, and it felt like I was on the homestretch, my motorbike broke down. Stuck in the middle of nowhere, and still soaking wet, I had no choice but to start pushing. It took almost an hour before I came across the first sign of civilization—a farmhouse. It was getting dark when I pushed the bike up the long, dusty driveway. A farmer came out to greet me, and I explained my situation. He couldn't have been more helpful. Once inside, he fed me soup and allowed me to sleep on his floor that night—quite the contrast from spending the previous night in the lap of luxury, but definitely better than the alternative of having to spend the night outside and alone.

In the morning, the farmer loaded my bike into his truck and took me to the mechanic shop, which was about fifteen minutes away. The mechanic looked over the bike and told me, "You got a broken piston ring." He wanted to charge me a lot to take the motor apart, but I didn't have that kind of money.

"Give me the tools. I'll do that myself," I told him.

I pushed my bike into the corner of the garage, and using his tools, disassembled the motor. The cylinder was seared from the broken piston ring, but I was able to pull out the piston, so the mechanic could replace the piston ring. I might have bitten off more than I could chew. It took about four or five hours to get the bike up and running again, and the last thing I wanted to do was to get back on the road, so I did the next best thing and asked the mechanic to direct me to the nearest train station. I got there and loaded up my bike on the next train to Paris. My wool clothes were still wet from the day before. I was entirely out of money, and hadn't eaten in ages, but I made it to the city.

It was 10:00 p.m. when I arrived at Walter's estate. My uncle wasn't home, but his teenage stepdaughter, Marina, was there. By that point, my French was much stronger, and I could speak Argot, so we could talk while she made me some scrambled eggs to eat. I don't remember scrambled eggs ever tasting so good!

I quickly settled back into my old routine at the estate and the office. At times, I inadvertently found ways to get on my uncle's nerves. Outside of work, Walter loved to entertain, and when I was staying with him, I would attend the dinner parties he hosted. One night, I was among twelve guests for a party with an elaborate spread—the servants were even dressed up. I was quiet at first and politely listened to the conversation at the table. When I finally felt that I had something to contribute, I proudly made a statement in French (I can't for the life of me remember what it was) that caused the entire room to go dead quiet. Suddenly, all eyes were on me. After a few seconds of silence, Walter got up from the table and motioned for me to come with him. I followed him into the kitchen, and once we were out of earshot of the guests, he let me have it. "You have no idea how much you just embarrassed me, and you have no idea what you just said! We're going back in there, and you will not open your mouth for any reason whatsoever." I didn't realize that I had said anything wrong. Whatever it was I said, it must have had some double meaning, or it was slang because I had never seen my uncle that angry.

Walter eventually calmed down and things returned to normal, but I didn't have much time to relax. Six weeks after returning to Paris, I received my next assignment, which was quite different from my time in Aix.

•••

There was a damp, stone shed in a small town in the central part of France called Cholet, where a group of ten young women stood at a long table all day long grading French angora rabbit wool. Cholet was a town located at a crossroads—literally. On one corner there was a mechanic's shop. Across the street, there was a restaurant bar with two rooms above it. That was about all there was to the town back then.

Cholet was where Walter shipped me off to next. He had been buying a lot of French angora from a co-op based in Cholet, and it was important to him that I learn how to grade angora wool as part of his business. I had sold the motorbike back in Paris, so I boarded a train to Cholet. Upon my arrival, I rented one of the two rooms above the restaurant.

For eight hours a day, I stood on the cement floor of that shed, grading angora at the table with the young women. They would talk, but I kept to myself when at work. Even when I left the shed, the angora was stuck to everything. It was like I had Velcro all over my body. I'd stand in the shower, and all the white wool would rinse right off only for me to return home covered in it the following day. I would come back from work, shower, eat dinner, fall into bed, and wake up and do it all over again. That was my schedule, except for the weekends.

I slowly began to assimilate. After a few days of living above the restaurant, a few townspeople acknowledged me with a slight nod. After a week, some said "Bonjour" and even "Ça va?" ("Are you okay?")

The first weekend in Cholet, I wandered into the mechanic's shop across the street from the bar. I can't remember his name, but as the only mechanic in Cholet, he was usually working on tractors and other farm equipment. On that Saturday, he was sitting on a box outside the large door to his shed, surrounded by four farmers. I walked over, said, "Bonjour," and they invited me to join them, which I did.

A nineteen-year-old American kid was a novelty in that town. The more I talked to the people, the more I realized that nobody there had ever had a genuine conversation with an American before. The only Americans they crossed paths with were the ones who came to visit central France, and those Americans apparently never made any attempt to understand or appreciate the culture; they expected everything to be just like it was back at home. During those conversations, my first instinct was to get defensive when they criticized Americans and America. Instead, I tried to explain to them how most of the Americans they encountered didn't know the language, so they couldn't effectively communicate, which made it difficult for anyone to understand and appreciate the French culture.

All of the locals I met in Cholet were good to me personally, and through my conversations with them, I learned how the French interpreted Americans as being impolite and vice versa. In many ways, they were both right, but hearing the French locals describe what they viewed as the "Ugly American Syndrome" really helped me to understand the empathetic nature of travel. I hadn't realized it before, but growing up in Woodbridge, New Jersey, my perception of the world had been myopic. After two weeks in Cholet, I started developing empathy for a foreign culture and non-Americans in general. While traveling, I became more sensitive and learned to appreciate the different priorities and sensitivities of a new culture. I was even picking up on the subtle differences of neighboring regions, such as Aix-en-Provence in the south of France, and Cholet in the center of the country. In hindsight, those experiences provided the foundation which would later help me attract clients in Belgium, Kenya, Australia, Pakistan, and India.

My uncle's business wasn't confined to France. The mill I had worked at in Aix produced raw material that was then shipped to Pattons & Baldwins Mills in Matlock, Derbyshire, England, where the raw material was blended with English wool and made into high-quality sweater yarns. Northern England was the third location my uncle shipped me off to.

The mill manager was named John Broome, and I stayed with him and his family for three weeks. He lived in the beautiful little country town of Matlock. John's house was on one side of a valley with a stream running down the center and castle ruins on the opposite hillside. In the morning, we'd walk to work at the massive plant. John was the largest employer in the town of Matlock, and he was well respected among everyone there.

My focus during that trip was only as an observer to see how the raw product from Aix was used. I roamed the factory floor and watched what everyone was doing. On the weekends, I got to tour the beautiful English countryside. Sometimes, John would take me into Nottingham and once showed me a historical site called the Seven Sisters, which was like a minor Stonehenge. Four of the girls who worked at the plant were in a singing group, and a couple times, they invited me to a nearby town to listen to them perform. Most of the plant workers were of Scottish ancestry, so I was exposed to and learned to appreciate the cultures of both Northern England and Scotland. Those lessons learned in Cholet were reinforced as my awareness of cultural nuances continued to grow.

After three weeks, I returned once again to Paris and my uncle's estate. I went back to work at the Paris office. I would ride into the office with Walter at 8:00 a.m. and return home with him at around 5:00 p.m. My duties were expanded to include various administrative tasks, and I even started transferring money around, but mostly I seemed to be getting in everyone else's way. I wasn't competent enough to really do anything worthwhile. Needless to say, I was beginning to outstay my welcome.

I didn't know how much longer I was going to stay in France, or where I would go next, but I was starting to get bored. Living with my uncle felt isolating. He was on the outskirts of the city, which meant that I was so far out of town and away from the bars, discos, and restaurants that I didn't get to meet many people my own age. It was lonesome for me over there. I didn't have any friends in Paris, but I did spend a lot of time talking with my friends back in New Jersey from Walter's office phone. Even Walter was gone much of the time. He was always at a business meeting or away traveling, so I was often left to fend for myself. One weekend, I went into town and up to his office, where I started writing a book, something about the real story of an American in Paris. As I looked out the fourth-floor window and watched the people below, I tried to concoct a narrative, but I didn't get very far.

When alone and in the city, I would go to this little restaurant on Godot-de-Mauroy, where UAP (Universal Animal Products) was located, and sit at a communal table. Some of the prostitutes from the street would also come sit at that same table. Several spoke a little English, but by that point, I was speaking much better French, so we were able to communicate. I had gotten to know several of them very well during my varied times in Paris. A few had been concubines of the United States military officers during WWII when they were in their teens and early twenties. I couldn't help but feel for them as they talked about being left behind when, after the war, the officers returned to their families in the States. Just like the guys from the French Foreign Legion, these women also looked out for me by shooing away the traffic warden, so my uncle's car wouldn't get another ticket. Even with their help, I still managed to accumulate over $1,000 in parking tickets during my stay.

Before my uncle could ship me off again, I learned from a friend, who worked for the draft board back in New Jersey, that I might be getting drafted. I was growing bored in France, yet France was a much more appealing alternative than going off to fight in Vietnam. But the choice was clear. After eleven months in France, it was time for me to return home.

3

TAKE TWO

WALTER BOOKED A STEERAGE-CLASS TICKET for me aboard the SS *United States* for what would be a five-day journey home.

I arrived at the Port of Le Havre by train from Paris to find complete chaos. A massive amount of people were trying to board the ship. It was noisy, and it smelled awful, but waiting in line was made more tolerable because there was an extremely attractive girl next to me. She had a bewildered look on her face, so I asked, "Are you as confused as I am?" We struck up a conversation as we waited to board. That helped to pass the time, and once on the ship, we went our separate ways.

In steerage, I shared a cabin with three other guys. I had the top bunk in one of the two bunk beds. The guy on the bunk below me was a Sikh from India who would tie his turban in the mornings. I had never seen anything like that before, and it fascinated me every time. Luckily, we all got along, and I settled in for what I thought was going to be a long, boring trip, but I was wrong.

On the first evening, I was approached by an officer who asked if I had a jacket and tie with me. I did, since I had been traveling with all my worldly possessions. I had no clue what was going on, so I asked, and was told that I had been invited to a special dinner. He told me to change my clothes and follow him. He then led me through the heavy, watertight door that separated steerage from the rest of the ship. Apparently, the young woman I spoke with while boarding the ship was a beauty pageant contestant and the current Miss England, Pamela Searle, who was traveling alone. Once we set sail, everyone started hitting on her, and that became a problem. I must have made quite the impression because she asked that I serve as her escort to an event that evening. Of course, I agreed. Was I going to say no?

I joined Pamela in first class for a dinner hosted by the captain. It wasn't romantic, but we enjoyed each other's company and had a lot of laughs, usually at the captain's expense. Luckily, I got to see her again because, on two additional nights, I was asked to leave my hovel and join her for dinner with some of the other passengers in first class. When the boat docked in the United States, we said our goodbyes, and that was the last time I ever saw her. It turned out that she went on to be an actress who starred in a few films.

I wouldn't go so far as to call myself worldly after spending only one year abroad, but I definitely had a different perspective following my return to New Jersey. I had grown up, somewhat. There was also a new reality that I was forced to face, one that I didn't give much thought to while living in France—the Vietnam War. Of course, I knew of the war, but I wasn't proficient enough in French to read and understand the French newspapers, so I wasn't closely following what was going on. Most of the coverage I could understand focused on how France was the first country to fight the Communists in Vietnam. That proved to be a military disaster for France. By 1959, Vietnam was quickly becoming America's war. The conflict was relatively new for the U.S., and it wouldn't get intense until the early 1960s, so it hadn't been on my radar at all. I was preoccupied with the work that I was doing for my uncle and living in the moment. Like most nineteen-year-olds, I wasn't thinking much about the future. I hadn't even thought about the prospect of having to fight in Vietnam until my friend called me with the news that I might be drafted. It was a wake-up call that scared the hell out of me. Once the shock wore off, I asked my friend what I should do, and he told me that the Army Reserve was still an option. That involved six months of active duty including two months of basic training. After active duty, I would be in the ready reserve and I'd run the risk of being called up anytime for the next five and a half years. I would be taking a chance, but it was much more appealing than going into the Army for two years of active duty. Had I returned to college, I could have delayed the draft prospect, but school was still not a high priority at that time, so I enlisted in the Army Reserve.

I was faced with a new set of challenges, but I didn't dwell on the negative. That's not me. It isn't now, and it wasn't back then. I had three months before I left for basic training, and I wasn't going to sit around, so I got a job working for a landscaper. I was part of a three-man crew who cut grass and raked leaves. I tried to enjoy the little time I had. My brother and I had never had a close relationship, so I didn't get a very warm and cuddly homecoming from him, but my mother was happy to see me. I got calls from friends welcoming me home, and it was really nice to get a visit from my high school girlfriend, Donna Carrol, who stopped by and told me that she had missed me while I was gone. With only three months before reporting for the Army, I couldn't really settle in, or get too comfortable back in Woodbridge.

In November of 1960, I boarded a bus in Perth Amboy, New Jersey, with a bunch of other recruits for a trip down the road to Fort Dix, which took less than an hour. When we piled off the bus, it was just like you see in the movies. We were met by a drill instructor who welcomed us in his own way, by screaming at the top of his lungs. He wasn't the most imposing guy, he was all of five feet four, but from that moment forward, there was never any question as to who was in charge.

The next step was processing, and I went to the back of an extremely long line to get my hair cut. When I sat down in the chair, it took the guy less than a minute to shave my head with an electric razor. He moved on to the next soldier, and I was sent down the line to get my physical. I touched my toes, got my testicles checked, and kept moving on down the line to a long shed. I was handed a duffle bag. The next non-com looked me up and down to eyeball my measurements and gave me a set of fatigues. As I kept moving down the line, more non-coms kept stuffing more clothes into my duffle bag, so by the time I reached the end, the bag was completely full. I was put into a platoon of one hundred guys, taken over to the two-story barracks that had been built during WWII, and assigned a bunk. I had only been there for a couple of hours, but it was a whirlwind. I was already numb.

The very next day, the sergeant assigned me to be the platoon leader, which involved me relaying orders from him to the rest of the platoon. I can't think of anything that I might have done to stand out. I had only been there a day, but I may have appeared to be a little more mature than the other guys, so I got the nod, which was fine by me.

Basic training was different every day. It didn't help that New Jersey was hit with one of the worst winters in years, so it was freezing cold the entire time. We'd have to go outside and brave the elements for exercises. I was in great shape and could physically handle whatever they threw at us. At 179 pounds, I was probably the lightest I'd weighed since I was ten years old. I learned how to fire an M1 and throw grenades. After spending half of the day outside in the cold, they'd take us all to a classroom inside a Quonset hut that was boiling hot. Still wearing our bulky outdoor winter clothes, we'd have to squeeze to fit into these tiny chairs with the desk attached while we listened to lectures on military tactics and etiquette. We were given handouts and had to take notes, but I constantly found myself having to hold on to the desk because it was so hot in there that I struggled to stay awake. One time, I fell asleep, tipped over, and took the entire desk down with me.

The barracks at Fort Dix were all made out of wood, so at night we had what they called "fire watch." Someone had to stay up to make sure that the barracks did not catch fire. Two weeks into basic training, I had made friends with a small group of guys from New England—two from Maine, three from Massachusetts, and one from New York. Our days may have been active, but none of us were anxious to sleep, so when one of us was on fire watch, we'd all stay up and talk, sometimes until 4:00 a.m.

That was my introduction to Ayn Rand and *Atlas Shrugged*. I had not read the book and had no knowledge of the material, but a lot of these guys were heavily into Ayn Rand. Never having been a part of philosophical conversations before, I did a lot of listening and asked questions about the concepts. I was once again being exposed to a different perspective.

Many of those conversations revolved around the topic of success. *How do you evaluate whether or not you're successful? What does success mean?* I started to see how success had less to do with where you were in the pecking order and more to do with how you could contribute to society and your community. Success went beyond the self. It wasn't just about money, but more about what you did with that money. It was fascinating to see how different guys from different parts of the country viewed success because there were clear cultural differences in what was prioritized. The kids from Maine thought differently than the guy from New York.

Through those conversations, I started to develop my own opinions about quality of life, financial success, and one's responsibility to society. I realized that financial success came with a certain cultural responsibility. Given how busy I was at the time, I didn't get a chance to read *Atlas Shrugged* to better understand these ideas until years later. Now, I make it a practice to read that book once every ten years, and I've read it about five times now.

All of our discussions and relationships in the platoon were civil. Overall, we were a pretty mellow group, but there was one time when someone got out of line. One guy apparently stole a piece of jewelry from someone else. It wasn't valuable, but it was important enough, so that once we discovered who the guilty party was, we did something about it, a blanket party. That involved throwing a blanket over the guy while he was sleeping and beating the ever-living hell out of him. We roughed him up pretty good, and since he was covered by a blanket the entire time, he never knew who participated in the beating. After that, there was never a need for another blanket party in our platoon.

As basic training progressed, I began to notice the distinct difference between those in the platoon who participated in the fire watch discussions and those who had no interest in the concepts. The primary difference was education. I wanted to pattern myself after those who had an education. I may have failed out of Rutgers, but I was reasonably confident in my intelligence. I was pretty much a straight-A student in high school, so I knew that I wasn't stupid and that I could succeed in college if I had another shot at it. But first, I had to complete my obligation to the Army before I could even begin thinking about college.

Field maneuvers were held during the final week of basic. That involved trekking into the woods to perform various exercises, like mock ambushes and fighting scenarios. It just so happened that it snowed like crazy that week, and it was seriously cold. On the first day, we must have walked a good five miles into the woods. That may not sound like a lot, but when it's twenty degrees out, and you're walking through snow that is eighteen inches deep, it's damn far. We stopped at night to eat, and together with the guy I buddied up with, we set up our two-man pup tent for the night. It was so cold that I couldn't go outside to pee, so when I woke up in the middle of the night, I had to kneel down and pee out through the tent flap.

I had been camping enough times as a Boy Scout to have picked up on a few tricks. First, I made sure to bury the tent flaps in the snow so the wind wouldn't blow under them. More importantly, I knew enough to put my boots in my sleeping bag. That way, when I got up in the morning, they'd be warm. Some of the other guys didn't have the same forethought. As a result, their boots were so frozen hard in the morning that they struggled to get them on and wound up with severe blisters after wearing frozen boots.

After two months of basic, we were all given an assignment for the remaining four months of active duty. One of the options was being shipped off to Fort Leonard Wood in Missouri for Advanced Infantry Training. That's where you learn how to be a fighting soldier. It's intense. Luckily, I dodged that bullet. I didn't even have to leave Fort Dix because I was assigned to the Adjutant General Corps. My job was to administer the battery of aptitude and intelligence tests the soldiers took when they entered the Army. It didn't get cushier than that, so I had no right to complain. Plus, it afforded me some exciting opportunities.

That year, the United States served as the host for the CISM (International Military Sports Council) World Boxing Championship. Five weeks into my AG assignment, the boxing competition was held at Fort Dix. Soldiers from all over the world arrived at Fort Dix to compete. That meant the Army needed interpreters and escorts, so they announced a temporary duty assignment for anyone who spoke a foreign language. I spoke French (sort of), so I submitted my name and was chosen to serve as the guide and interpreter for the three-man team from Qatar. The team was comprised of a sergeant, a corporal, and a private, and they didn't speak any English.

It was a 24/7 assignment, so for a couple of weeks, I was with them from early morning until they retired at night. They were Muslim. I was Jewish. That didn't make a bit of difference to them or to me. We all became great friends, and I got to learn about the Muslim religion. They would say their prayers multiple times a day, and always facing Mecca. I had never seen anything like that before. Back when I worked as a waiter at Admiral Farragut Academy, some of the other employees would come with me to synagogue on Fridays and then on Sunday I'd go with them to church. That exposed me to various aspects of Christianity, but this was the first time I was exposed to the Muslim religion, which proved insightful.

We were all on a tight schedule, so our activities were limited. They ate, trained, and slept—that was about it. We didn't have time for much of anything else, except for once when I was able to take them off base for a little while, though we didn't get to have too much fun because the Army was very strict about anyone leaving the base. I never did get into the ring with any of those guys. My military boxing career consisted of only one fight when I squared off against a heavyweight, but that fight didn't last very long. I didn't land a single punch and got my clock cleaned royally. I can only imagine what any one of those guys on that team would have done to me. The private was one hell of a fighter. He was only a bantamweight, but he was tenacious and speedy, so it was no surprise that he won a bronze medal in his weight class that year. It was great to have a break from my tedious routine for a couple of weeks, but what stood out about that experience was the insight I gained into a different culture. It was stimulating to be around those guys, and it extended my international exposure.

In 1958, while on a trip to the mountains with her friend Ann Feibush, my mother met a man named George Blacher. George was from Connecticut and owned a pair of bicycle stores with his brother, Irv. The romance between George and my mother blossomed, and they were married in 1960. Woodbridge was only thirty-five minutes away from Fort Dix, so I was able to come back home for the wedding. George was a nice guy, but we didn't have much in common. He was the kind of guy who got most of his information from *Reader's Digest*, so deep discussions were difficult, but as long as he was good to my mom, we got along fine. My mom then moved to Stamford, Connecticut, where she and George settled down. After that, I didn't have much reason to return to New Jersey. However, since my father and grandmother were both buried in Woodbridge, years later I would make it a habit to stop by the cemetery and pay my respects whenever I was driving back and forth between Dallas and New England.

With my active duty coming to an end, I knew that it was time for me to give college another shot. One thing that I learned from the Ayn Rand discussions was that once you get an education, nobody can take that away from you. It's yours for your entire life to do with what you want. Not only was a college degree a rite of passage that made you part of an elite group, but it provided a pathway to a career. I had grown fond of my uncle's lifestyle in Paris, but it required a certain amount of money to live like that. The only way that I could think of earning money at that time was with a college degree leading to a corporate job.

The guys in my platoon from Massachusetts talked a lot about Northeastern University in Boston. Back then, Northeastern was the second-largest cooperative education program in the country, next to

Drexel University. Today it's the largest. Cooperative education basically meant work-study, so instead of going to school for four years, with time off in the summers, like at a traditional college, Northeastern had a five-year program. You had no time off. You'd go to school for two semesters, work for a semester, and then come back and go to school. That pattern continued for five years, so when you earned your degree, you already had two years of actual work experience under your belt. Since I was already three years behind my high school friends, Northeastern's intensive educational and work experience program appealed to me. However, I still had no clue what I wanted to do. I had no burning desire or objective at that point. The one thing I did know was that I didn't want to be an astrophysicist. I had learned a lot while working with my uncle in France and developed an interest in international business, so I figured co-op education might give me a chance to explore different occupations. I took leave and traveled up to Boston, still in my Army uniform, and interviewed with the admissions department at Northeastern. Shortly after, I learned that I was accepted to the business school and would begin in the fall of 1961.

When I was discharged from active duty in the Army Reserve, I went back to work at the landscaping company to earn some extra money before I started school. Once enrolled, I took general business and economic classes. I really liked those classes, and I did well, too. Things were different this time around. For one, I was personally embarrassed that I had been thrown out of Rutgers. Combine that with the awareness that an education was necessary, and I was motivated to see what I could achieve when I applied myself the way I thought I could.

Since I applied late, there was no dorm space available for me. When I inquired about housing, I learned there was a fraternity house where I could live as long as I pledged, so that's what I did. Once again, I found myself sharing a room with three other guys. We had two bunk beds. I had one of the bottom bunks, and Paul Therian had the top bunk above me. He was from Rhode Island and was a devout Catholic who said his rosary every single night. The way he clicked his beads used to drive me crazy, so for my own sanity, at Christmas, I bought him washers to put between the beads when he said his rosary. We were close enough friends that he was a good sport about the gift.

The fraternity was fun until Hell Week rolled around. That's when they took the pledges and forced them to do all kinds of stuff. There was one brother who I didn't get along with at all, and tensions only escalated between us at the start of Hell Week, when he took a pair of scissors and gave me a reverse mohawk. It was god-awful ugly, and I was furious. All of us pledges made it through Hell Week, but when they asked if I wanted to become a brother, I was so pissed off that I flat out told them no.

There was another fraternity made up of several guys who also had been in the service called Phi Alpha Rho, so I moved into an apartment with them on Hemingway Street in Back Bay near Northeastern. Pledge week for most fraternities involved hazing and physical abuse, which I was okay with up to a point, but Phi Alpha Rho sent their pledges into New York City and gave them a series of unique tasks to complete.

I was put in a group with four other guys, and we drove down to New York City from Boston in a van. While we were going through our checklist of tasks, which included stealing a park bench from Central Park and a street sign (I took 3rd Avenue, and it's still in my garage), we were not allowed to shower, shave, or change into clean clothes. After three days, my final task was to have my picture taken with the maître d' of the Four Seasons Restaurant, one of the most exclusive restaurants in the city. And we had to take the picture right in front of the bronze plaque with the Four Seasons logo on it that was located right outside the restaurant, so the brothers would know it was legit.

That evening, when our van pulled up to the restaurant, I stepped out and, smelling awful and looking like a bum, introduced myself to the doorman. "Hello. My name is Fred. What's your name?"

He looked at me as if I were crazy. "My name is Fred, too."

"Hi, Fred. I'm going to need your help. I'm pledging a fraternity in Boston and need my picture taken with the maître d' outside the restaurant in front of the plaque."

There was a long pause, and then he burst out laughing. He thought it was the funniest thing he ever heard. "Wait right there. Let me see what I can do."

He went inside, and while we were all waiting there on the curb, the patrons entering the restaurant gave us the strangest looks as they sidestepped us on their way in. A few minutes later, Freddy returned with the maître d', and we took the picture. Our group managed to check off every single item on our list. I went back to Boston, became a brother, and continue to enjoy the PAR Brotherhood to this day.

My experience at Northeastern couldn't have been more different than my time at Rutgers. In addition to joining the fraternity, I was in the top two of my entire class, top of my class in the business school, was elected to the student council, and named class vice president. I have always been outspoken. Some people didn't care very much for what I had to say, but enough did that my section put me up for all of these positions in student government. I feel that I helped to get a lot done for my class while being a good representative for the business school and chairman of the student-faculty committee.

I was pretty efficient when it came to making things happen, but one thing that I didn't have was money. I had no income, and after I pissed away my tuition at Rutgers, my mother wasn't too keen on the idea of supporting me at Northeastern, so I applied for financial aid. The Travelli Scholarship was awarded to students with good grades who were active participants in extracurricular activities at the university. In my second year, I was fortunate enough to be awarded a Travelli Scholarship with full tuition for the remainder of my studies, and that gave me some much-needed financial breathing room.

Everything was starting to click, but I still wasn't any closer to knowing what it was I wanted to do with my life. When it came time for me to go to work, my first co-op job was at a major Wall Street brokerage firm called Bache & Company, where I was assigned to back-office operations. Since the job was in New York City, and I had to pay for an apartment and the increased cost of living, I didn't have much extra money lying around for anything else. After one semester of working on Wall Street, I knew that I had zero interest in that line of work. My second job at Royal Globe Insurance in Boston wasn't much better. I spent my entire semester there processing claims. I don't think I could have found a more boring job if I had tried. In the 1960s, students did not have much say in their choice of co-op jobs, but they do today. Sometimes the jobs were a good fit, and sometimes they were not.

Finally, at the start of my third year in 1963, an exciting opportunity came my way. There were seven of us from the business school who were assigned to be the first group of co-op students to work for the Ford Motor Company in Detroit. I was ecstatic because this was really a plum job, and Ford was paying good money for us to go to work there. After I finished my final exams on Friday, I packed every worldly possession I owned and traveled as part of a convoy with the other guys. We cut across Canada's QEW, and arrived in Detroit at 8:00 a.m. Saturday morning. All seven of us met in a coffee shop, got a newspaper, and found a house to rent. That weekend we moved in, and we all prepared for our first day of work on Monday morning.

4

THE MOTOR CITY

HE WASN'T A BIG GUY. He was probably only five feet eight, but he was intense and very serious. He didn't have a great sense of humor, and he didn't tolerate any BS, but more noticeable to me than his stature or demeanor was his crystal-clear ability to communicate, his meticulous attention to detail, and his demand for accuracy. That was why Joe Cappy was named the Marketing Services Manager for the entire Lincoln-Mercury Division of Ford Motor Company when he was only in his mid-thirties. It's also why he would become one of the most influential early mentors of my career.

Among the guys I traveled with to Detroit, I was the only one who was assigned to the Lincoln-Mercury Division. The others all worked in different departments at Ford, such as the engine plant, the assembly plant, operations, and public relations. From the first day, when the woman from HR walked me up to Joe Cappy's office, I immediately knew that this co-op job was going to be different than my previous two. At Lincoln-Mercury, I would be doing real work. I wouldn't be stuck in the back office filing papers, processing claims, keeping records, or running errands. I would be working closely with Cappy. My desk was in his outer office, and he had to walk by me several times a day when he was in town, so it was difficult not to interact with him. I started getting real insight into the business from the man who was running the entire marketing services program for the whole Lincoln-Mercury Division, which was why I kept that co-op job for my final three years of college.

I didn't have much free time during that first semester in Detroit. Monday through Friday, I was up at 7:00 a.m., and into the offices at Lincoln-Mercury by 8:00 a.m., and worked until 5:30 p.m. To make some extra money, I took a second job working as a bartender at a folk bar in Highland Park, featuring music from emerging stars like Gordon Lightfoot. I didn't make much in tips. First off, most of the people came for the music, and there was a cover at the door, so they were less inclined to buy the drinks from the bar, which weren't cheap by any means. Also, this was the 1960s and tipping wasn't as customary back then as it is today. Still, I wasn't very good at schmoozing with the customers and coaxing a tip out of them. The guys that made money behind the bar were the ones who would either carry on conversations with the patrons or embarrass them into forking over a sizeable tip. That wasn't me. However, I still made it work. The money I made at the bar was enough to cover my apartment and living expenses, which allowed me to put my salary from Lincoln-Mercury in the bank. In what little free time I had left, I'd go out with the other guys I roomed with. We spent a lot of time at the Rooster Tail, which was a bar right on the Detroit River. I was always doing something, so the days flew by.

Luckily, when the semester ended and I headed back to Boston, I was able to return to the apartment on Hemingway Street with the rest of the fraternity guys. Back in Detroit, I had learned how to put the culinary skills I'd acquired while cooking for Nicki at the bar in Aix to good use by becoming the cook for the entire house. I took on those same duties in Boston, but that task proved more difficult than it sounds because I wasn't living with small guys. One of the brothers, Max St. Victor from Haiti, was a fullback on the football team who was six feet five and 260 pounds, so you can imagine how much he ate every day.

Working for Ford came with its perks. Since I was an employee, I got a great discount on a Ford Mustang Fastback that I purchased in 1964 during my second semester in Detroit. It was a beautiful car that had just come out with a standard transmission, and a lively 287 Ford engine. I was clocked by a Canadian Mountie at more than 100 miles per hour on my first return trip to Boston in that car. Each semester, I would return to Detroit with the same group of guys who accompanied me the first time, but the problem was that we couldn't return to the same house. We kept having to find a new place to live each time out, which proved to be challenging at times because we never knew what kind of living arrangements to expect when we made the trip.

Cappy was delicate with me during my first semester in Detroit, but when I returned to work for him the second time, I was more of a veteran, so the gloves came off. He gave me more responsibility, and I was put in charge of compiling reports that contained information he required to run his department and make crucial decisions. I would come to find out, sometimes the hard way, that there was zero margin for error.

The first large study he asked me to do was on the installation rate of the different custom options for Lincoln-Mercury cars. Back in the 1960s, the cars didn't come with all of the same standard features they do today. For example, a car radio was just one of several items that you could get when you ordered a new car. I started my research by creating this vast matrix of the installation rate of all the different options by the make and model of the car.

It all sounds incredibly dull on the surface, but it's quite fascinating when you're forced to take a closer look. That report allowed me to calculate the profit margin for each option. So, if someone ordered a car, I could plug in those numbers and come up with exactly how much profit the company would make when producing that car. For example, I learned that 98 percent of all vehicles produced by Lincoln-Mercury had a radio installed. A few other options had very high installation rates as well.

When I showed all of this data to Cappy, his recommendation was that options that had an installation rate of 95 percent or higher should be standard on the automobile and priced in. Not doing that was cost-ineffective for the company. But Cappy didn't just look at the surface level numbers, he went deeper by breaking down the different combinations. So, he knew that if someone ordered power steering, they would be more likely to order power brakes, which were priced separately at the time. He had it down cold. I had never been around someone who could look at the same data from a variety of perspectives to gain insight into the product. Cappy also looked closely at trends, so he could better predict how customer choices would evolve. Not only did he make things easy to understand, Cappy almost made them seem obvious. The conclusions he was able to draw from analyzing all of the numbers were impressive.

That was the first time that I heard about the Pareto principle, which basically means that 80 percent of the effects come from 20 percent of the causes, or in our case, 20 percent of the products would give us 80 percent of the profit. We could then look closer at that 80 percent of our product that was producing only 20 percent of the profit to make sure that we weren't overextending our product line and offering too many choices, since some choices are actually taking away profitability and revenues because of higher costs. From a business perspective, that analysis gave me great insight.

All of the special orders for Lyman-Peterson limos that were assembled for politicians and other celebrities went through Cappy as well. I was asked to create reports for those requests, which were often outrageous and commonly included various bulletproof material. The bulletproof material made sense for certain heads of state and politicians, but I was shocked to learn what some celebrities wanted to put in their automobiles.

I managed to pick up some tips that would later help me out as a consumer. I now know never to buy a new car in the first one hundred days of production. Designing an automobile is complicated, and even after you start to produce the cars, making sure all the parts fit correctly is extremely difficult. Some parts and options work well, but others have to be modified. Some create noise, others have access problems, and some create installation problems because of the way they have to be put into the automobile on the assembly line. The ECRs (Engineering Change Requests) seem almost endless at first, but all of those production changes are usually introduced in the first one hundred days from the start of production.

With this in mind, the second study Cappy had me do involved compiling the cost of various ECRs. This was a list of the necessary manufacturing changes required to improve how parts were put into the automobile during the first one hundred days of production. Once again, I put together a comprehensive study that summarized all of the requests we received in a full year and organized it by make and model. This was no easy task because the sheer volume of changes that had to be introduced, especially in a new model, was mind-blowing. What we discovered was that the design of a relatively few of the specific components caused almost 80 percent of the installation or production problems. Lincoln-Mercury was then able to go back to the assembly plant to focus on those problems and eliminate a significant number of ECRs.

When I created those reports, Cappy read them thoroughly. There was absolutely nothing I did that he didn't notice. He once made me rewrite a marketing report that was going to Ford corporate and the head of Lincoln-Mercury eighteen times until it was up to his satisfaction. He wasn't averse to telling me when something wasn't the way he wanted it. It got to a point where he wouldn't even read the whole thing. He would start from the beginning, but as soon as he came across a mistake, or felt that I had drawn an improper conclusion, he would give it back to me and say, "This isn't right. You need to write it again." That's what I did, and each time I brought it back to him, we got a little further into the report. It had to be clear and concise—he didn't want people using a lot of words.

Joe Cappy's professionalism, work ethic, and attention to detail were impressive. He was very hands-on when it came to showing me how things worked. He was a great tutor and one hell of a mentor, but he definitely had his own way of doing things that didn't follow the conventional mentor-mentee model. He insisted that everyone who worked for him, or even just worked around him, possess that same mental discipline. He refused to accept mediocrity. If you weren't willing to learn, you were gone. He did not suffer fools and wasn't afraid to call people out when they weren't performing. When he dressed me down, which he did frequently, it was between us. He was hard, but he didn't embarrass me. He corrected me in a way so that I learned something. It was extremely effective because that made me want to do better, and when I wasn't able to satisfy him, I was more frustrated with myself than I was with him for calling me out. I wasn't the only one in the office who felt that way. Everyone worked damn hard to gain his approval and acceptance. There were a couple of times where I got an "attaboy" from him. He didn't give many of those out, so it made me feel really good when that did occur.

After working for my uncle in Europe, and meeting many influential people, I've never been impressed or in awe of someone only because of the title on their business card. What impresses me about an individual is their character, how they accomplished what they did, and how they treat those around them. And I was in awe of Joe Cappy. He knew his job inside-out, and his talent was with numbers, particularly the ability to look at numbers in a different way than most people and to truly understand what those numbers meant. I learned that by seeing the conclusions he drew and the decisions he made with the data I compiled. It's no surprise to me that he went on to have an incredibly successful career. After spending twenty-six years at Ford, Cappy became the President of American Motors in 1982, then Vice President at Chrysler, and retired as CEO of Dollar Thrifty Automotive Group in 2003 at the age of sixty-nine.

Slowly, the number skills of Cappy's began to rub off on me, and I could see things differently. He helped me to realize when I really understood the numbers and when I didn't. Sometimes, you just look at a set of numbers and get it, but you can never achieve that level of certainty if you never take the time to put the numbers together, take them apart, and then put them back together in a different way. That's the only way to truly understand the benefit and consequences of decisions made based on those numbers. I might not have recognized it until years later, but with that skill in my tool kit, I had the confidence to speak up and challenge those around and above me when I knew what I was talking about.

I wasn't the only one who worked for Joe Cappy in the same capacity. Since Northeastern's co-op program operated on a model that had me alternating between semesters of working in Detroit and going to school in Boston that meant someone else had to work at Lincoln-Mercury when I was at Northeastern. The program was divided up into an A division and a B division, but I never met my counterpart in the B division who worked for Cappy when I was in Boston. I would have loved to have been able to compare notes and talk with that guy about his experience in Detroit. I wonder if he was able to get as much out of the experience as I did.

One thing I particularly enjoyed about working for Lincoln-Mercury was that I wasn't stuck in an office all day. The job was always different. I had a variety of assignments over three years that provided me with opportunities I could have never anticipated. I was asked to audit the Lincoln-Mercury Division racing program. I got to meet and work with Carrol Shelby, who created the Ford racing program and modified cars for Ford. When I was there, he had just built the 427 Cobra, which I got a chance to drive. I got to go to the Indy 500, something I never would have thought about attending on my own, but it turned out to be an incredible and eye-opening experience. I was sent out to various cities throughout the Midwest to audit dealers' warranty and policy claims. I once found myself in the Quad Cities in Iowa when it was four degrees. It took thirty minutes to defrost the inside of the car before I could even drive it. Every day was an adventure.

Lincoln-Mercury put together a slew of promotions during my time there, the most memorable being when they released a family car called the Comet. To prove the car's reliability, they drove three Comets as part of a convoy from the tip of South America all the way up to Alaska. I was responsible for gathering data on all the financials and writing reports for Cappy, so he'd know that the funds were being properly spent. It was a promotion with a lot of moving parts, literally. Traveling with the convoy was a press plane with a bunch of automobile reporters. A stunt like that sounds good on paper, but since I had a peek behind the curtain, I could see how it wasn't practical. Some of the roads and bridges were washed out in South America, so we had to pay to have these cars flown to the next road or ferried across the river. It wasn't always pretty, but the people on the ground did what they needed to do to get the cars to Alaska, where they were met with much fanfare. It was really fun to be a part of that promotion.

My personal life felt equally chaotic at times. During my second semester at Northeastern, I met Ginny Rizzo in one of my classes. She thought I was an obnoxious smart-ass, and she did have a point, but she must have seen some positive traits in me as well because we started dating. I left for Detroit, and her co-op job was in New York with the World's Fair, so we didn't see each other that often. And once she started living in the city, she met a guy and started dating him, but we always remained great friends, and we still are to this day—she would later attend my wedding.

Meanwhile, because of my student council duties, I frequently found myself in the office of Roy Woolridge, who was the Dean of Cooperative Education and the President of the Cooperative Education Association. While waiting, I always chatted up his secretary. Her name was Solveiga Kalnins, which was a Latvian name. I called her Sol. I eventually asked her if she would type up a paper for me since I was using the hunt-and-peck system on my typewriter. We started dating soon after that. She was a year older, and had a daughter from a previous marriage, but she wasn't a student. She was a full-time employee and had a good job with a lot of responsibility.

My relationship with Sol was casual at first because I was leaving town every other semester, but things grew more serious in my senior year. While I was getting to know Sol, I had a management class with a Northeastern football player named Dwight "Bucky" Grader. He told me a story about how he worked with the guy Sol was dating and would have to listen to him constantly complain about some yahoo named Fred Brodsky, who was trying to move in on his girlfriend.

Bucky was having his own relationship problems at the time with his girlfriend, Liz, who had a violent temper and serious anger issues. He used to invite me over to dinner as a way to keep the peace, but my presence didn't always help. During one of their heated arguments, Liz threw an entire bowl of spaghetti at him, and the red sauce splattered all over the wall, just like in a movie. In an attempt to stay out of Liz's way, Bucky and I would often play tennis or go drinking at a Boston bar called The Gainsborough. There we'd have "dimeys," which were a glass of beer for literally a dime. After college, Bucky and Liz got married. I'm godfather to his second son. We continue to remain good friends and have been strong competitors in racquetball, squash, and golf (until my back went out and I had to stop playing), but Bucky still competes aggressively.

When I returned to Detroit for my last assignment, I was there for six months and shared an apartment with Paul Kerrins. I had learned a lot about corporate business my previous three years at Lincoln-Mercury, but I wasn't sure if that was something that I wanted to be a part of in the future. It was a huge corporation, and there were a lot of politics that went on behind the scenes with the Ford family and the various other powers that be. One thing I did notice when speaking to co-workers in Detroit and students back in Boston was that very few people understood international business. It simply wasn't on anyone's radar in the 1960s. My experience with Walter in Europe stimulated my interest in the international aspects of business. It turned out that the University of Michigan was one of the few schools in the country at that time that had an international business program. Since I had been living in Detroit long enough to be considered a resident, that's where I applied to get my MBA, and I was accepted.

Sol and I had been talking about getting married after graduation, and that was still on the table when I got my diploma. Once I was accepted at Michigan, the plan was for her to move out with me. We even looked into getting family housing, but there was nothing available. Well, nothing available that I could afford, at least. I didn't have money, and she had a good job back in Boston, and a child to take care of, so we kept running into roadblocks. Even though we didn't get married, we still stayed together for a little while, but we were on borrowed time, and the relationship would fizzle within a year before we parted amicably.

After five years at Northeastern, I was ready to complete my education and get on with my life, so I wanted to get my MBA as quickly as possible. Luckily, I was able to get advanced credit for all of the basic business classes I had already taken during undergrad. That turned out to be my salvation and would allow me to finish sooner. At Michigan, I took courses in international finance, international marketing, and international operations. It would be total immersion, and I would have no time for extracurricular activities because I'd be taking twenty credits per semester, so I could graduate in ten months. Nothing was going to deter me from the plan.

Graduate school was a fresh start, and Sol remained back in Boston, but I wasn't completely alone. David Smith was a fraternity brother of mine at Northeastern who enrolled at the University of Michigan along with me. We had agreed to be roommates and were assigned to a two-bedroom apartment just off campus. David and I shared a bedroom—we put our beds head-to-head—and the second bedroom was assigned to two other guys we didn't know, but who were also enrolled in the graduate programs at Michigan. Paul was getting his PhD in clinical psychology, and Alan was getting his PhD in radio and television production. I found it ironic that Paul, the future clinical psychologist, was the strangest guy I had ever met. I never saw him sit down. Never. Even when he was eating, he'd always be standing up. Whenever he went into the bathroom, for whatever reason, he always turned out the lights. It was bizarre, but he proved to be harmless, and we all got along that year without incident.

My only real break that year was a brief trip to Paris for my brother's wedding. We may have not been close, but when I learned that he was going to get married, I felt that as his older brother, I should be there. I wanted to show up in Paris at the wedding and surprise him. I found a cheap fare, but I didn't have a passport. I applied for a passport and booked a flight, but as the wedding grew closer and I still didn't have my passport, I started to get nervous. The guys who worked at the Ann Arbor post office got to know me pretty well because I started showing up there every day, asking about this passport. It finally came in on the day that I was supposed to leave, so I called ahead to the post office. One of the guys was waiting outside to hand it off to me on my way to the airport. I made it on the plane and arrived in Paris without anyone knowing I was there and without a plan. I just randomly showed up at the home of my new in-laws and couldn't have been more warmly received by the family. When I showed up at the wedding unannounced, my brother was completely blown over. It was a great surprise and a wild two days, but I had to immediately get back to the grind.

School was going well, and the living situation was satisfactory, but I could see that I was going to run out of money before I graduated. I didn't have any time to work a job, and I couldn't ask to borrow from my mother. At Northeastern, the Travelli fund was my primary source of financing for four years, so I took a chance and reached out to the trustee in charge of the fund. It was a complete shot in the dark, but I asked if there was any way that they could help with my expenses, and it worked! I told them that I needed $2,000 to finish my MBA, and they sent it to me without question. When I graduated and tried to repay what they sent me, they wouldn't let me give them a dime. I was told, "If you're ever in a position to help others, do it." Before I got off the phone with them, I promised myself that's exactly what I would do.

After six full years of school, I had built what I perceived to be the educational foundation I needed. I had come a long way since working in the toll booth on the New Jersey Turnpike with Johnny Tatola, where we spent our days hustling girls headed for the Jersey Shore, and nights partying on the beach. I may have been reluctant to go to France and work for my uncle seven years earlier, but that turned out to be the start of my transformation. Those conversations I had with the locals in Aix and Cholet opened me up to an entirely different perspective. I was slowly changing and growing with each new experience. That evolution continued in the Army, progressed through Northeastern, and was expanded during my work with Joe Cappy. I was gathering building blocks and adding to my tool kit, but I didn't know what I wanted to build yet. I wasn't any closer to knowing what it was that I wanted to do with my life, but I knew for sure that I wanted to move on. More specifically, I wanted to get out and work so I could make some money. I was tired of living on a shoestring budget and eating an unhealthy diet of Burger King Whoppers and Morton's mac and cheese, which I could get three packages of for one dollar.

Many companies came to the University of Michigan to interview graduating MBA students. The school had a great reputation for placing students in consumer product marketing jobs. Procter & Gamble was a big recruiter, but they didn't interest me at all, and neither did McKinsey & Company Consultants. I interviewed with them to be a consultant, but I didn't like them, and apparently, they didn't like me either because I didn't receive an offer.

I started to realize that if you work hard and have ambition, it's incredibly difficult to keep your work separate from the rest of your life.

The challenge is finding a career path that complements the lifestyle you want to live. For me, that involved specific criteria that fit my MBA in international business. Unfortunately, that also limited my options. I had learned to love travel, so I needed to find a job that involved travel. I didn't want to be stuck in one spot as an analyst or a consultant.

I ended up getting four or five offers, but there were only two that I seriously considered. The first was an analyst position at Trans World Airlines, which came with the allure of responsibilities around the world and international travel. The second opportunity was with Touche Ross & Company. Touche Ross was one of the big eight accounting firms and was number three at that time in terms of size. They had three divisions—audit, tax, and consulting. They had also just acquired a small Spanish-Italian consulting firm and wanted to use that firm as the basis for expanding their consulting operations throughout Europe. If I accepted the offer, I would be the Manager of Consulting Operations for Europe. That role would require me to live in Madrid and Rome, while primarily helping Touche Ross's existing European clients minimize problems while maximizing operating opportunities.

I spent a long weekend considering both offers and came to the conclusion that Touche Ross provided me with more potential for growth. The chance to live in Europe also turned my head, so that's the offer I chose to accept. However, things wouldn't turn out quite as expected.

5

GETTING MY FEET WET

I **ARRIVED IN NEW YORK CITY** for the planned six-month orientation, and quickly signed a six-month lease on an apartment on 83rd Street, just off 1st Avenue. After my co-op experience, I knew how to quickly find a place to live, negotiate a lease, and move in. I didn't have any assets or furniture that required moving from one place to another, so that made things much easier. Everything was going well until I showed up to work on my first day.

Pat Loconto was my new boss. As soon as I arrived, Pat and the head of the New York office sat me down. "We have good news, and we have bad news," Pat said. "The bad news is that the company we bought had three sets of books instead of two. We are divesting ourselves from this company, so there is no role for you to play in Europe."

I was devastated, yet still held out hope that something might work out in my favor.

"The good news," Pat continued, "is we just got a contract to develop the criteria for the Manpower Development and Training Act recently passed by Congress. We're going to do the cost-benefit analysis for this program across the United States and design a reporting system to inform Congress on the benefits and costs of the act in the different states. We want you to be a part of this exclusive five-member team, working directly with the United States Department of Labor in Washington, D.C."

Pat tried to pitch it as an exciting opportunity to be a part of a select team that was doing important work for the government, but I wasn't buying it. Pat was heading up the team, as partner-in-charge, and he didn't seem too excited either.

When the shock wore off, my head was spinning, and I was beyond frustrated. How could an international CPA firm not know the true financial condition of the firm they had acquired? I was aware that many European companies had two sets of books, one for internal management and one for the tax authorities. However, that third set of books Touche Ross had suddenly discovered represented the real financial condition of the consulting firm, and they painted a much grimmer picture than the hyped set of books originally presented.

The opportunity to live in Europe, the extensive variety of the job, and being responsible for the growth of consulting services in Europe were the reasons why I took the offer from Touche Ross. After the long and arduous application and moving process, I had spent the past few weeks filling my head with visions of traveling around Europe. It all came crashing down in just a couple of minutes, but there was nothing I could do. I was stuck. I had way too much student loan debt and couldn't afford not to have a paycheck coming in while I looked for another job.

My orientation was completed in six weeks, not the original six months, and then the team made its way to Washington, D.C. Touche Ross covered the cost of my New York City apartment as part of my compensation, and I found an efficiency apartment in the southwest part of D.C. on 11th Street.

Immediately, I began to butt heads and clash personality-wise with the newly appointed team manager, Dick Levine. His style of managing was to impose himself and try to intimidate those working under him, while encroaching on some of the duties that were ultimately my responsibility. I felt that I knew my job and what I was doing better than he did, so I was not very receptive to his approach. That led to some heated arguments that had to be refereed by Loconto.

I was not doing what I wanted to be doing, and I did not like the job at all. I resented being sold on a position in Europe that never materialized. However, there was a silver lining. At twenty-seven years old, I was finally making money for the first time. My salary was $47,000 a year. I received a per diem while living in D.C., and my New York expenses were covered, so my salary was disposable income. I used that money to pay off my student loans as quickly as possible and spent most of the rest. I also slipped into a social routine outside of work. While frequenting the bars in the Foggy Bottom area of D.C., I met a young lady named Patty, who was an analyst at the CIA, and we quickly started dating.

The job also involved some travel, and one trip sent me out to Eugene, Oregon, which was a small town back then. I'd work with the city government during the week, and on the weekend, I traveled around the state all by myself. The sights were beautiful in Oregon. One weekend, I decided to stay at a ski resort in Mount Hood where there happened to be a ski instructors' convention going on at the time. The participants loved to party, so the weekend proved to be a lot of fun. On a separate trip, I went into Portland and happened to pop into a club to watch a young, up-and-coming group called The Supremes that featured a singer named Diana Ross. The club had artificial stalactites hanging from the ceiling. It was a ratty, cave-like atmosphere, but the vocal group was incredible, and even though nobody had ever heard of The Supremes, it was clear to everyone there that we were witnessing something special.

While Dick Levine may have made what was a difficult situation back at the D.C. office even worse, Pat Loconto was a pleasure to work with. I may not have liked what Pat was saying when he broke the news to me about the job on my first day of work, but he was very personable, and during my time in D.C., I became close friends with him and his wife, Wanda. He was only a few years older than me, and in his early thirties, but he already had two young boys, both under five years old.

Patty and I invited Pat, Wanda, and the kids all over to dinner one night, and the two boys were crawling all over the floor of my tiny apartment. I didn't have time to cook a proper meal that night, so I had gone out earlier and bought individual, pre-made steak and kidney pies. All I had to do was heat them up. It wasn't a gourmet dinner by any stretch, and it didn't help that no one liked steak and kidney pie. That became a running joke for years and it was a story Pat and Wanda would not let me forget for a very long time. Luckily, I had bought a couple of bottles of nice wine, so the evening wasn't a complete loss.

We always knew the assignment in D.C. was temporary, and after eight months, it came to an end. We all returned to New York, where I was assigned a couple of new jobs. It was a lot of filler and busywork, but some were interesting opportunities. One was to help Tiffany's evaluate their marketing program. I felt underqualified for the job at first, but in the end, I was able to make a positive contribution to Tiffany's marketing strategy by helping them better understand some of the problems they were experiencing with their current approach.

The most interesting assignment I had was to develop a lecture for the American Management Association (AMA) about the challenges and opportunities of doing business internationally. The AMA organized different programs and offered lectures to its members. Touche Ross supported the organization by volunteering speakers, and they recruited me because they knew about my experience in France and England. I wasn't even thirty, but I had more experience when it came to international business than most. This was also back in 1969 when a lot of people didn't even have passports.

During these hour-long lectures, I spoke a lot about what I had been exposed to while in Europe. The challenge of doing business overseas wasn't only overcoming the language barrier; there were cultural differences that could lead to potential issues as well. Something as simple as a facial expression or gesture can easily be misinterpreted because it doesn't mean the same thing in other cultures as it does in the United States. For example, in Japanese culture, a person may shake his or her head, and you'd think that person is nodding in the affirmative, but that's not necessarily the case. In some cultures, it's considered rude to show anyone the bottom of your shoes. Some words and phrases have double meanings, and that can have consequences when you speak, just like the situation I found myself in when I spoke up during my uncle's dinner party in Paris. I was able to weave in some personal stories, and that's part of what made the lecture experience so enjoyable.

In attendance at one of my lectures was Norman Brust, who was the Vice President of Marketing for ITT WorldCom. Afterward, he hung back and told me that he had enjoyed the lecture and appreciated my insights. He then asked if I would consider taking another job. I didn't know who he was at the time, but I didn't have to think twice before telling him, "Hell, yes!"

Pat Loconto knew that I was frustrated and not doing the type of work I wanted to be doing. I had never made that a secret, so my decision to leave after almost one year didn't come as a surprise to him or anyone at Touche Ross. About six weeks after returning to New York from D.C., I resigned from my position and went to work at ITT World-Com. ITT was also located in New York, so I was able to extend the lease on my apartment on 83rd Street. That worked out well because I didn't want to leave. There were twelve apartments, three on each floor, and I was one of only two guys in the entire building, so it was a fun place to live.

In 1969, ITT was the parent company, and WorldCom was a major subsidiary of which WorldCom U.S. contributed about 50 percent of total WorldCom revenue and profit. WorldCom owned other telephone companies in South America, Puerto Rico, and Europe. It was still the era of telex machines, but the industry was advancing to combine voice and data protocols. When I began working at ITT, the industry was also in the midst of a paradigm shift from mechanical signal switches to electronic switches. That meant all of the old mechanical rotary switches were being replaced by electronic digital switches to make for fewer moving parts.

It was a tumultuous time, both in the industry and the world. The United States was in the middle of the Cold War with the Soviet Union, and ITT operated the hotline between the White House and the Kremlin. The connection came through our New York office. This was a hardwired connection that would allow the leaders of both countries to be connected immediately in the case of an emergency. It was tested every single day. It wasn't a revenue producer for the company, and I have no idea if it was ever used during my time there, but it was still fascinating to be aware of the role WorldCom played.

Every once in a while, I had to deal with the press, so when a request for an interview came in from a Japanese newspaper called the *Asahi Shimbun*, I was picked to sit down with the reporter. It's customary in the American business world to ask the guest if he or she wants something to drink, so that's what I did when I sat down with the female reporter. She asked for water, and I wanted a cup of coffee, so I asked my secretary, Stephanie, to get the beverages for us. We started the interview and it went well. I thought I represented the company in a positive light, but that didn't prove to be the case. What started as an article about mid-level management in the United States turned into a piece on how American managers abuse their employees by forcing them to do demeaning tasks, like getting coffee, which apparently Japanese executives don't do. From that moment forward, I knew that I had to be extra cautious when speaking with the press, especially the press from another country where there might be huge cultural differences when it comes to values and mores.

My bosses at WorldCom laughed about the article, and couldn't care less, but the corporate executives at ITT were a different story. They weren't happy, and I received a few direct comments about the article, but in the end, it didn't affect my position. My duties luckily involved more than press relations as I was afterward forever leery when talking to the press.

Tim Coles was the WorldCom U.S. Sales Manager, and one of my early assignments was to help him coordinate a trip to the National Sales Meeting in Bermuda for all thirty-six WorldCom salespeople across the country. I called American Airlines, and they sent New York salesmen John Capozzi and Vince Caminiti to help me make the arrangements. These two guys were the consummate entrepreneurs who showed up at their sales meetings with attaché cases loaded with their marketing swag. Pens, key chains, plaques, ashtrays—you name it, they had it. They were also good at what they did. Things got complicated when trying to coordinate travel to Bermuda, and it took over a month to finalize all of the arrangements, but everything worked out and the meeting went off without a hitch. That wasn't the last I heard from John and Vince.

Normally, John and Vince dealt with executive secretaries and women in corporate travel departments because they were the ones who ultimately made the decision on which airline their executives would use. American Airlines went so far as to create a special program called "The Fair Ladies of American Airlines." That program involved a trip on American's dime and, of course, John and Vince would serve as escorts. They were the perfect men for the job.

Right before Christmas in 1968, John and Vince asked me to join the group as an additional escort for the thirty women who signed up for the trip that year, and I gladly accepted. We flew to Puerto Rico on a Friday and stayed at a great hotel. On Saturday, we flew to Saint Thomas for a five-hour shopping trip, and then returned to New York on Sunday. Everything was first class, and we had a serious good time.

After that, I became close friends with John and Vince, and we'd see each other socially on a regular basis. When John retired from A.A., he went on to become a very successful entrepreneur and writer who made a fortune writing books that American Airlines would help distribute, such as *Why Climb the Corporate Ladder When You Can Take the Elevator*; *If You Want the Rainbow, You Gotta Put Up With the Rain*; and *A Spirit of Greatness: Stories from the Employees of American Airlines*. When Vince retired after twenty-eight years, he moved over to Delta Airlines to become the first senior executive who Delta hired from outside of the company.

My major task during my first year at ITT was to coordinate the marketing section of the massive, company-wide five-year plan. Each operating division provided its own comprehensive plan. This report was the primary basis for all of ITT's corporate planning. It was over three hundred pages long and included sections that provided an overview of problems and opportunities, personnel, revenues, expenses, and a plan for each service or product that each ITT subsidiary offered.

It also provided a forecast for each service or product and how it would contribute to the overall revenues for the division in the following year.

My work on the marketing section attracted the attention of ITT WorldCom U.S. General Manager Valerian F. Podmolik, who promoted me to be his executive assistant. I had never spoken to him during my first year when I worked for Brust. Podmolik was a man of few words, but everyone said he was tough. He was all business—a guy who you seriously did not want to piss off. On my first day of working for him, he called me into his office to compliment the work I had been doing. He told me, "If you can do the job I want done, you have a great future ahead of you."

I didn't want to disappoint him, and asked, "What do you want me to be able to do in six months and then in twelve months?"

"Open my mail" was all he said.

I thought he was joking, but what he really meant was that he wanted me to be able to take care of the office while he traveled the world, working on technological improvements and coordinating relationships.

Podmolik moved me into an office next to his, and our secretaries shared an alcove nearby, but this wasn't a job that ended when I left the office. It never really ended. I learned to keep a pad and a recorder right next to the phone by my bed because Podmolik had absolutely no compunction whatsoever about calling me whenever he had the urge. It didn't matter where he was in the world or what time of day it was in New York. The more confident Podmolik became in my ability to handle the issues at WorldCom, the more he was able to travel, which translated into more late-night calls.

I quickly picked up on the way Podmolik worked and, just like I had been with Joe Cappy, I was very impressed with the way he approached his job. When all of the department heads would meet,

Podmolik was very astute at being able to seek out the details that were significant and disregard the rest. He didn't waste his time with anything trivial. Those meetings were weekly, but then once a quarter, the Executive Vice President of ITT Corporate, Ted Westphal, would come in to review our operation. Podmolik was the one who prepared the report for Westphal. It wasn't long before I took on the responsibility of preparing those reports.

Podmolik oversaw the United States operation, which was the major hub for the ITT WorldCom system. For example, calls from Europe to South America would be routed through WorldCom New York. WorldCom also owned the Puerto Rican Telephone Company and a series of other communication companies all over the world. Every week, the GM of each of these country's operations would send in what they would call the pink sheet report. It was a highly confidential and encrypted report about anything going on in each GM's country that could affect not just WorldCom, but ITT. It reported on political unrest, treasury function, terrorist or insurgent operations in the county, financial problems, banking situations, and all types of highly classified info. One of my jobs was to summarize those pink sheet reports and pull out anything of significance, so Podmolik would be aware and take action as necessary. Reading and summarizing the pink sheets provided me with a significant amount of insight into situations all over the world that I would have never otherwise been privy to.

I worked hard, and it paid off. One year later, I was promoted to Director of Long-Range Planning and Financial Controls. My secretary, Stephanie Zubietta, was excellent, but I also needed an assistant to better help me understand the technical components of the operations Podmolik wanted me to be responsible for. That's when I hired Vinny, a WorldCom employee with twenty-five years of experience, who proved to be invaluable because he was tied to all of the union guys in operations. Vinny was my contact with the rank and file on the operating floor. Whenever I needed insight into that aspect of the company, Vinny was the guy who would get me the info and help me better understand what was going on.

Stephanie, Vinny, and I formed a great team, and together we became incredibly efficient at getting everything done when Podmolik was out of town, which was frequently. The more I was able to handle tasks without any negative repercussions, the more latitude he gave me. Only one time did I test the limits of that freedom, and it occurred on St. Patrick's Day when I took Vinny and Stephanie to the bar across the street for a three-hour lunch. I was drunk by the time I came back, and it turned out that Podmolik had been looking for me. He pulled me aside and said, "Go in your office, close the door, and don't talk to anyone. If you ever show up drunk again, I will fire you." That was the only conflict I ever got into with him.

Most of my time was spent at work, but when I wasn't in the office, I learned that the people who lived in my apartment building were a lot of fun. I started dating Gretchen, who lived in the apartment next to me. She and her roommate were TWA international flight attendants. They would often come back from their trips with baguettes, cheeses, and wine from Paris, which they shared with me. Whenever I was really trying to impress a date, I'd bring her by the Four Seasons because Freddy the doorman still remembered me from my fraternity stunt. In the years that followed, I only ate at the Four Seasons a few times (it was god-awful expensive), but Freddy would always call me Mr. B, and that would make a good impression on whoever I was with.

Everything at the office ran smoothly until a year after my promotion when the Communication Workers of America (CWA) went on strike when their contract expired. It didn't help that the expiring contract coincided with the transition to electronic switches because that called for personnel changes and a reduction of operating personnel. As Director of Long-Range Planning, it was part of my job to implement the strike plan, which meant that I also got to sit in on these meetings. That's where I received a crash course in how union negotiations work at WorldCom.

Paul Toomey was the head of HR for WorldCom, and he was the one who led the contract negotiations with CWA. On that first day of discussions, there were three of us from WorldCom in the conference room and about eight representatives from the union. We were grossly outnumbered, but in order to show that he wasn't intimidated, while also expressing his absolute disdain for the president of the local union, Toomey put his feet up on the conference table. When I saw him do that, I almost fell out of my chair. In Europe, I'd learned that it's incredibly impolite to show the bottom of your shoes to anyone, and there Toomey was with his feet directly opposite the union president. The conversations began by discussing the grievances of the union, and they cited their demands, but Toomey would periodically pick his nose and do other things to demonstrate that he really couldn't care less who was there and what they had to say. I had never seen a professional behave like that before. His style was most certainly unique.

It was no surprise that WorldCom and the union could not come to terms. The union's response to the breakdown in negotiations was to call a strike, and on their way out of the building, douse all of the rotary switches with hairspray in an attempt to disrupt WorldCom's business. It was left up to the non-union supervisors to manually clean each switch. That took several hours, but luckily, we were able to get it all done and restore reliable communications.

When you're dealing with communications, you can't afford an interruption or degradation of service. I was ultimately put in charge of implementing the comprehensive strike response to secure the systems and the operations. There was a book on how to deal with a strike that was passed down to me, and while implementing the plan, I didn't divert too far from the book.

Things got heated. There was a picket line outside the Worldcom headquarters building and it was not a good idea for any of us to cross that line. We had dorms set up for us at the office, so we wouldn't have to leave. I was even assigned a bodyguard, but there was never a moment where I feared for my safety. In the end, it was all normal union negotiations, and the strike ended after three days.

While the strike may have ended, things didn't quite return to normal. Corporate was under pressure to improve its operating results and share price. Once the new deal with the union and operating side was finalized, an edict came down from ITT corporate mandating a reduction in personnel by 10 percent. That meant laying off two hundred employees, and Podmolik put me in charge of firing forty-two of them. And I had to do that in a single day.

I was terrified when I sat down with the first employee, but after speaking for about ten minutes, the guy got up and thanked me for not being nasty about it. That made me feel a little better about what I had to do, but that feeling didn't last long. The reactions that followed were all over the map. Some people cried, others threatened me, a few became hysterical, and one guy even fainted. He actually fell to the floor. Having to sit down with forty-two people and speak with them for ten minutes each about how they no longer had a job was a horrible experience. It was probably one of the most difficult things I've ever had to do when dealing with other people in business. I needed a few drinks at the end of that very long day.

My duties may have expanded while working for Podmolik, but I could never escape the responsibility of coordinating the five-year plan for WorldCom. I had originally helped assemble the marketing section, but I was now responsible for coordinating all of the sections of the plan and producing the final product. The plan itself was sophisticated for its time, and the same format could probably still be used today to great effect. It was very predictive. When you're dealing with technology and assets that either have to be built or need space provided to them, you have to project into the future and figure out how to provide all of the various elements within a multi-service company. For example, power requirements coming into the WorldCom building were constantly adjusted for the increasing traffic and services being provided. Coordination with the City of New York and the New York Telephone Company required extensive lead time to insure adequate power and communication cabling.

Much of my final two years were spent writing what would become the core of WorldCom's long-range planning strategy. A key component of that plan was a section called "problems and opportunities," which allowed me to appreciate the significance of both identifying and developing strategies to minimize problems and maximize opportunities. That section necessitated significant operational focus, but when it came to some of the engineering areas, I felt out of my depth. I'm not an engineer or a computer person by any means, so that part of the report proved to be more difficult for me. WorldCom and the other telecommunication companies were experimenting with voice data communication where bursts of data were blasted in the gaps of voice communication. Much of our speech involves blank space and WorldCom was developing technology to transmit significant amounts of data in those gaps. In order to better understand these new technologies, I relied heavily on Vinny and the CFO of WorldCom to make sure the information going into the report was accurate.

Once the WorldCom department heads and management signed off on the draft report, Podmolik and the other WorldCom companies would present their five-year plan to ITT Corporate—Chairman Harold Janeen, Executive Vice President Ted Westphal, and all senior functional officers. The physical report books were printed in-house, and when you're trying to print fifty three-hundred-page briefing books, things can go wrong. Naturally, on the day we were to present at the ITT corporate offices, which were located in a different part of the city, the printing department was late in getting everything together. They cut it as close as possible. Podmolik and I were already waiting in the limo when they finally loaded up the last of the books and we headed to the meeting.

The ITT boardroom was massive and could fit about fifty people. At the front, Janeen and Westphal sat with the rest of the ITT corporate staff—the company logo in ITT blue on the wall behind them. Podmolik and the other presenters filled out the rest of the seats at the oval table. Everyone had microphones in front of them, and there were four clusters of four speakers, each in the open center of the table. Three large video screens were set up to show the speaker and presentation slides. Behind the table, there were chairs for the support staff, which was where I sat. Since I had coordinated the preparation of the report, I sat behind Podmolik. I had my briefing book ready, which included support for every major point in the report, so when someone asked a detailed question of Podmolik, I could provide him with the exact data he needed to respond. Not only did they have questions, they had very good questions. From the draft documents provided in advance, the extent to which the ITT corporate staff had prepared was impressive. They had really digested the information down to the key elements and wanted to make sure that the problems were being mitigated and the opportunities were being maximized. At this meeting, significant time was spent discussing strategies to mitigate the potential consequences of Chile's attempt to nationalize the telephone company, then owned by WorldCom, and Puerto Rico's attempt to increase the tax on the Puerto Rican Telephone Company, also owned by WorldCom.

Podmolik was a fascinating guy and I had a much more interactive relationship with him than I did with Joe Cappy. Both men had the ability to examine numbers, but Podmolik had a unique skill set. While Cappy could evaluate numbers and history, Podmolik was more forward-thinking in the way he could predict trends and consequences. He had a rare ability to draw conclusions from numbers that nobody else around him was able to do. He could look at endless pages of information and then pick out the one or two items that either didn't fit the picture or weren't properly supported. That skill was what put him at the top of his field. Watching the way that he worked gave me further insight into how to test the significance of numbers and evaluate relationships among numbers, especially cause and effect. While certain revenues might be interpreted as strictly volume and price, I learned from him that things aren't necessarily what they seem. The volume could be the result of normal communications or spiked by a unique event somewhere in the world that resulted in increased transfer traffic.

Unlike many bosses, Podmolik didn't mind being challenged, and I had a good time engaging him in these conversations. After my experience working with Cappy, I was confident enough to argue with Podmolik when I knew what I was talking about. Nobody else argued with him that I was aware of. Sometimes I was right, and sometimes I was wrong, but he respected my opinion because I too had become very good at looking at numbers and understanding the relationships among numbers. And that's one of the reasons why I believe he promoted me twice in three years. That education began with Cappy, but I'd like to believe that I acquired a certain level of intuition with numbers from Podmolik. There is no way that I could have paid for the education I got from him.

I had turned a corner professionally and was becoming much more confident in my skill set. I was thirty-one, and only out of school for a couple of years, but I was able to interact with major corporate leaders at all levels without experiencing any angst or discomfort. I was getting good with numbers and learning how to effectively communicate both verbally and in written reports. However, I didn't realize any of this at the time. Getting thrown out of Rutgers had a significant impact on the way I evaluated myself. It might have given me an inferiority complex that I was still trying to compensate for and that made me feel like I needed to prove to myself that I wasn't stupid. Despite all that I had accomplished, I still felt that I was behind and needed to play catch-up. It's also probably why I worked myself into the ground at WorldCom.

Podmolik was constantly traveling, and after three years, I just got tired of being awakened at all hours of the night by his telephone calls. I was exhausted and burned out. I needed a break. Also, I was already the Director of Long-Range Planning and Financial Controls, so there was no way for me to move up, except by going to corporate. I knew that it was time for me to leave, so I resigned. Podmolik was disappointed to see me go, but he also recognized that it was time for me to move on. Since starting at Northeastern, I had been going nonstop for ten years. It had been one hell of a ride, but I was ready to take a break. I didn't know for how long, and I wasn't sure what I would do next with my career. There was absolutely no plan. I was confident that I'd know it when I saw it or felt it, but for the time being, I needed to recharge.

6

COMING INTO MY OWN

WALTER HAD MOVED FROM PARIS to Majorca, Spain, which was quiet and remote, so that's where I decided to go to unwind and get some rest.

It was 1971, and my uncle was now sixty-one. He was married to Maria (wife number four), who was a beautiful and intelligent Swedish woman who spoke several languages. She was also thirty-two, only one year older than I was. I had always admired my uncle, but as I got older, I began to appreciate his lifestyle. In fact, I wanted to emulate it, except for the fact that I was a confirmed bachelor. He wasn't ostentatious. He never flaunted his wealth, but he enjoyed good wine, food, and cigars and always surrounded himself with interesting people. When I lived with him in Paris, he'd often invite me to tag along on business lunches, but there was an unspoken agreement that I was to keep my mouth shut because it was understood that I could not add anything worthwhile to the discussions. We'd meet with people he was trying to sell stuff to, and sometimes we met with people who were trying to sell him stuff. While I did not know the technical details of the negotiations, it was always evident to me when a deal was about to fall through, and the other party didn't stand a chance in hell of selling my uncle anything. If the proposal wasn't directly to the point, or if someone tried to BS my uncle, Walter would cut the discussion off abruptly. He did not suffer fools easily and if there was fluff or BS in the presentation, or the presenter was pompous, no business would be concluded. I would like to think that this characteristic is something I picked up from him and why I found myself gravitating back toward Walter at this critical juncture.

A lot had changed since I lived with my uncle in Paris more than ten years earlier. Not only had I earned my two college degrees, but I had worked for a major accounting firm, and one of the best-run conglomerates in the world, ITT. After ten years, the dynamic between Walter and myself had also changed. When I arrived in Majorca and settled in, he asked me to look over some of his recent business dealings and proposals, so that I could give him my thoughts. He was still doing the same type of work he did when I was in Paris—the importing and exporting of animal products. I was familiar with the business, but he had never asked my opinion before. My business acumen had advanced significantly, but as soon as we started dissecting the specifics, it was clear that I was not ready to make sound decisions in his business.

I stayed at Walter's house for the first ten days but soon realized that I wanted more independence, so I rented an apartment nearby on the beach in Santa Ponsa. We still spent a lot of time together. Walter was well known and well respected on the island. He was friends with both locals and expats. Whenever we walked into a restaurant, the staff always catered to us. Meeting all of these successful people helped me better understand and appreciate the good, bad, and ugly in some of them. I was starting to develop a value system that allowed me to not only read people, but also to determine which people I should cultivate a relationship with.

Miguel Pons was one of Walter's closest friends, and definitely someone I enjoyed being around. He owned the abattoir on the island. He was a big, fun guy, just like Walter, who loved to laugh and drink. Many nights, Miguel would join me, Maria, and Walter on his porch for a nice dinner with wine, and a lot of drinks afterward. I loved talking to Miguel because he grew up on the island and knew everything that went on there. We'd stay up late, and sometimes Miguel had to bite his finger to stay focused during his drive home. On the nights I didn't visit with my uncle, I'd often head to the bar around the corner from my apartment. There were even a couple of weeks Gretchen, the TWA flight attendant I dated back in New York, came out to visit. I didn't have anywhere to be, so in the mornings, I'd usually wake up around 10:00 a.m., have coffee on the beach while I read an English-language newspaper. Those days were hedonistic, but it was just what I needed to recuperate and recharge my batteries.

After about three months, I started to get bored, so I packed up my things and headed back to New York. I had made sure to keep my apartment in the city—I didn't want to have to look for another place to live, and I was having a really good time in that building. I immediately updated my resume and sent it out to over thirty headhunters. It was not long before I was approached by The Frey Group, which invited me to Chicago for a job interview. The Frey Group was made up of five companies and was owned by ARA Services (Automatic Retailers of America), a vending machine company based in Philadelphia, that had recently initiated an acquisition binge to grow the company and their stock.

I was hired as the Secretary-Treasurer of The Frey Group. Each of the five companies had their own CFO who reported directly to the president of that company, but also had to report to me on a functional level about their finances. My job was to compile the financials for all five of the companies. I reported directly to Alan Harvey, who was the President of The Frey Group and also the President of Dasol, the biggest of the five companies in the group. Harvey had recently sold Dasol, an assembly line specialist, to ARA Services for several million dollars. Harvey would forward my compilation and comments, along with his operating report, to Bill Fishman, the President of ARA Services in Philadelphia.

The Frey Group had been losing a significant amount of money for several months. Its reporting and financial control systems were pathetically antiquated. From a management accounting perspective, there was no way to understand why the operating losses were happening, other than the simplistic assessment that either revenues were too small, expenses were too high, or both. I worked until ten or eleven every night doing forensic accounting for all of the companies. That meant sifting through job bids, expense allocations, travel vouchers, and all the details associated with each company, so I could reorganize them and put them in the proper categories to see the true revenues and expenses.

After a few months of intense effort, I was able to determine that, of the five companies, Dasol was the primary cause of the losses. There had been no project cost accounting going on at Dasol at all. Harvey wasn't pricing his jobs out properly. I put all of this in a report that I gave to Harvey and explained to him why Frey was losing between $10,000 and $50,000 a month, which was a significant amount.

Not long after I submitted my report, I got a call from Pat Gibbons, who was Bill Fishman's executive assistant. ARA had been trying to figure out what was going on at The Frey Group, and why it was losing so much money each month. Pat wanted to meet with me, so he took the train up from Philadelphia. We spent a few hours in my office talking and continued our discussion over dinner that night. It turned out that Harvey had not given my report to Fishman and ARA. He was giving them his own explanation, but what he wasn't saying was that Dasol, his company, was the main problem. The other entities in The Frey Group were doing okay, but Dasol was almost entirely responsible for the group's losses.

Pat reported back to Fishman, who then invited me to ARA headquarters in Philadelphia to discuss what was going on. I took the train from New York and Pat escorted me into Bill Fishman's office when I arrived. The three of us sat down, and I found Fishman to be gracious and well briefed, as his questions were very direct and to the point. When Pat and Bill asked me about what was happening, I told them the truth. Fishman understood the issue and I left feeling that I had done a good job of explaining both the problems, and opportunities of The Frey Group, as I saw them.

Harvey may have been my boss, but it wasn't my job to protect him from Fishman and ARA. Harvey did nothing during my time there to generate any loyalty from me. He made his money when he sold Dasol to ARA, and I believe he was paid in full for the sale with no contingency buyout. It certainly appeared like he cared very little about what was going on in the office. When five o'clock rolled around, he would literally push past anyone in his way and head out the door, which left me to work primarily with his secretary, Peggy Burns. He was disrespectful to both Peggy and me, so much so that I nicknamed Peggy "PP" for "Poor Peggy," and still call her that today, fifty years later.

During ARA's evaluation of The Frey Group's performance, I became very close with Pat. He would come to New York on a fairly regular basis, mostly to visit his dad, Harold Gibbons, the Senior VP of the Teamsters International out of Saint Louis. Harold Gibbons was a tall, robust guy whom I met many times. I thoroughly enjoyed his company. He kept a suite at the Warwick Hotel that just so happened to have an open bar, so when Harold was in town, that's where Pat and I would go for a drink before we went out to dinner. When we were there, the phone would always ring off the hook with calls from people like Bob Hope, Frank Sinatra, and Sammy Davis Jr. Harold was a powerful and well-connected guy, and Pat, a Harvard MBA, grew up around all of that.

When it became clear that Alan Harvey was the problem with The Frey Group's performance, and his employment contract could not be broken, Pat recommended to Fishman that my talents be used elsewhere in the ARA companies. That's when I was reassigned to a construction management company called Morse Diesel, which ARA had also purchased during their acquisition binge. They were the largest general contractor of office buildings in the U.S. and were doing over $500 million a year in high-rise commercial construction. The Pan Am Building, 9 West 57th Street, Transwestern's headquarters, the United California Bank world headquarters in Los Angeles, and the Sears Tower in Chicago—not to mention numerous buildings in Manhattan on 3rd and 5th Avenues—were all being constructed by Morse Diesel. The company had also acted as construction consultants on the Sydney Opera House and Tour Montparnasse, the tallest building in Paris.

This was a big step up for me, and it came with a lot of responsibility. As CFO, I was tasked with improving the financial controls on the construction operation. That meant that I would be responsible for company accounting, project accounting for $500 million in construction projects, insurance, and IT. I reported to Chairman Carl Morse and President Harold Schiff.

I would be working out of New York, but Morse Diesel also had offices in Boston, Pittsburgh, Minneapolis/Saint Paul, Los Angeles, San Francisco, and Chicago. When I was hired, I went on a grand tour to all of the offices to meet everyone. The most memorable of those visits was to the Chicago office, where they were building the Sears Tower for Sears, Roebuck, and Co. After I met all of the executives, including the General Manager, Richard Halpern, I was handed over to the general superintendent, who said to me, "Let me show you what we do here, Fred."

I had no idea what he was talking about and couldn't have predicted what I was in for when he took me to the Sears Tower site; at the time, eighty-two of the 108 total floors had been built. We got into the construction elevator, which was like sitting inside a cage surrounded by an open mesh barrier on all four sides. On the ground level, it wasn't that intimidating, but the higher we climbed, the stronger the wind blew. By the time we reached the eighty-second floor, the wind was howling. We stepped off the elevator onto the partially constructed floor, and you could feel the building sway. I walked as fast as I could to the center of the floor, so I was away from the edge when the super yelled, "Come here, Fred! I want to show you something." He then grabbed a girder, leaned over the edge, and looked straight down, eighty-two floors. Even today, my stomach does flip-flops just thinking about that day. We were up there for fifteen minutes, but it felt like forever. I was so happy to get back into that elevator and head to the ground.

With more responsibility came more money, and the first thing I did was find a new apartment. I hated to leave my building, but I rented a beautiful apartment on 73rd Street, just off Lexington Avenue in Midtown Manhattan. The building was a pre-WWII building with a rosewood elevator and only three apartments on each floor. I finally had a full kitchen and a large bedroom that got a lot of sun and overlooked a garden. The living room was beautiful, and I had a nice fireplace with bookcases on each side, but the problem was that it was small, no bigger than twenty square feet. This was the early seventies and there were a lot of parties going on—it was a time when the hippie free-love lifestyle was in vogue. When we hung out, it was in groups of eight to twelve people, but if I wanted to fit that many people in my apartment, I had to get creative, thus was the birth of what became known as "the adult playpen."

I didn't have much room for furniture, so I convinced some of the Morse Diesel construction guys to build a three-foot high platform above the existing floor. It took up about 90 percent of the room and was flush up against three of the walls—we left a three-foot-wide walkaway along the remaining wall, which led to the bedroom and bathroom in the back. We also cut out a U-shaped notch in the middle of the platform where we placed a large, oval, glass-topped table, so I could seat six people for dinner. We covered the rest of the platform in carpet, and instead of chairs, I had about ten three-foot-square pillows for sitting. It was like a hookah bar. People would come in, take their shoes off, climb up on the platform, lie around, or sit at the large glass table. It was a great setup, and I had even given myself extra room for storage underneath the platform, so my creative thinking paid off.

I quickly got comfortable in the new apartment and my new neighborhood. There was a restaurant nearby called The Italian Steakhouse. I'd go in there on weekend afternoons for a cold beer before the other customers arrived and was in there enough to get to know the bartender, the manager, and the piano player, who was always practicing before the crowd came. The place may have been empty during the day, but at night it was a completely different story. It was packed. Limos would be lined up outside along 3rd Avenue, and sometimes there were bodyguards. That's when I put two and two together and realized that the restaurant was a mob hangout. I didn't know any of those guys, but it became my local joint. The food was incredible, and the service was superior. The manager, Michael, always made me feel at home when he called me "Mr. B" whenever I walked in the door.

Every so often, my mom would take the train down from Stamford, Connecticut, where she was living with George, and come to visit. She loved to meet at the Waldorf Astoria Bull and Bear Bar. I'd always take her out for dinner, and when I went to the hotel to pick her up, she'd be at the bar waiting, having already made friends with everyone there. At sixty, she was attractive, vivacious, and quite the character. Much like my uncle, she enjoyed good food, good wine, and she loved to travel. She was a lot of fun to be around. I wasn't as close to my brother Greg, who at that time had become spiritual and was living on a commune in upstate New York with his guru, Rudi, selling oriental art.

It was 1972. I was thirty-one years old and starting to enjoy a very comfortable and fun lifestyle. Barry Stern, a friend from New Jersey, was an assistant producer on Broadway. Through him, I met a group of actors, singers, and dancers who were performing in *Hair*. He also introduced me to Sally, one of the dancers from the Radio City Rockettes, and we soon began dating. I had a lot of time to be more social when working at Morse Diesel because, for the first time, I was working regular and consistent hours. I'd start at 8:00 in the morning, and work until 5:00 or 6:00 at night. I bought a motorcycle, a gold Honda 350, so I could travel from the city, especially over the summers when a group of friends and I rented a house on Fire Island. I enjoyed New York City and maintained my friendship with John Capozzi and Vince Caminiti from American Airlines, and the women from my old apartment building, including Gretchen.

It was my first time working for a construction management company, so I wasn't aware of standard practices. I had to learn the business. Construction, especially in a major city like New York or Chicago, involves interfacing with many difficult elements that can affect both the cost and schedule, such as police, fire, sanitation, public works, politicians, and unions. As the CFO of Morse Diesel, I interfaced directly with each project manager who dealt directly with each of these groups. I determined what to pay and what not to pay, as all cash and accounting was my responsibility, not just for the company, but to ARA and the owner of each building.

There are usually three to five key metrics that can determine the health of any business. In construction management, when any given project can last between two and four years, one key metric is the construction fee backlog and cash flow. Morse Diesel wasn't bringing in any new business, and they had not done any aging of their contracts to determine when the fee income would slow down. I put together an aging schedule, which clearly showed that fee income would drop significantly in about nine months if no new business was booked. I told them that they needed to start selling now to make up for the contracts that were maturing, and to maintain their cash flow. It was a serious problem, but one that neither Carl Morse nor Harold Schiff seemed the least bit concerned about. I'm not sure why they weren't, but the situation seemed eerily similar to what was going on at Frey with Alan Harvey because Morse and Schiff had made a lot of money selling Morse Diesel to ARA and weren't out there hustling for new business as they had before the sale. They may not have been concerned, but Morse and Schiff definitely weren't happy to hear what I was saying, and they knew they had to communicate what was happening to ARA, so my relationship with them became strained.

For the first time in my career, I didn't have a mentor like Podmolik or Cappy. Nevertheless, I remained comfortable and confident in my performance. Given the substantial pressure of maintaining a reasonable construction schedule, I had to set my own standards, and I grew very comfortable with my ethics. Evaluating new and different situations, and drawing conclusions that proved to be accurate, were more significant boosts to my confidence than I realized at the time. I learned that I was capable of walking into a completely different type of business situation, understanding the problems, dissecting them, and putting the pieces back in a way that would address those problems.

I believed that I had correctly evaluated the specific problems at Frey and Morse Diesel, but that didn't mean leadership was going to listen to me. ARA was ambitious in their acquisition spree, and they had bought companies with tremendous potential. Not all of those companies achieved that potential because the people running them made so much money in the sale to ARA that they lost the incentive to continue doing what had made them so successful in the first place.

•••

I had been at Morse Diesel for about fifteen months when I was approached by a headhunter who had been hired by Trammell Crow Company, at the time the largest private real estate developer in the United States. Trammell was looking for a CFO for his international operation. Given my MBA in international finance from Michigan and my role as CFO at Morse Diesel, I was the perfect candidate.

They flew me down to Dallas to meet with Trammell Crow himself; his CEO and former lawyer, Don Williams; and the CFO, Bob Glaze, at their offices in Bryan Tower. Over two days, I spoke with them and their regional partners, who laid out the details of their operation. In addition to developing the International Trade Mart in Brussels, they were developing projects in France, Germany, Italy, Spain, Brazil, England, Fiji, and Vanuatu and were looking at projects in Hong Kong and Singapore. Every project outside of the United States would be my responsibility. The position appealed to me because I would be getting back to what I really wanted to do, international operations and travel, so I took the job. I never realized how significant a decision that would be both for my career and my life.

I had grown very used to New York City and my exciting life there. By contrast, Dallas was dramatically different. This was back in 1973, and even though there weren't tumbleweeds blowing through the center of the city, there were plenty of areas that were dry, barren, and undeveloped. Some restaurants didn't even sell alcohol, but you could still bring your own in a brown paper bag. The local businesspeople would tell you how honest and religious they were. They'd smile, slap you on the back, but still be as aggressive and competitive as New Yorkers. The good ol' boy network in Texas took some getting used to, but after about two years, I realized that the only difference between Texas and New York was that the preliminaries took about five times as long in Texas.

The first thing I had to do was find a place to live. I got lucky and found a great apartment on Walnut Hill Lane, but it wouldn't be ready for a couple of weeks, so the company put me up at the Sheraton Hotel, which was right across from Trammell's headquarters in Bryan Tower.

There were no private offices at Trammell Crow. Everything was open, and I sat directly across from Trammell himself. He was a personable guy—very smart, charismatic, and gregarious. He took a personal interest in the people he worked with. One night, I was working late at the office because I wasn't able to pick up the new Pontiac Coupe I had bought until eight o'clock. Trammell came over and struck up a conversation and seemed genuinely interested in my situation. "How are you getting over there?" he asked.

"I was going to take a taxi."

"I'll drive you," he said. "I want to see your new car."

That's what he did. I rode over to the dealership with the head of the company, but he didn't just drop me off. We parked, got out, and he went inside to actually look over the car. "It's a beauty," he told me, and then he got back in his car and drove off. He really did have a nice way about him that was difficult not to like.

I didn't have much time to adjust to the new job. During my first week, I was thrown into the fire as the company was set to close on the purchase of a superblock in a new commercial area known as Azca in downtown Madrid. The sellers had already agreed to a price of $8 million, but when it came time to close, they asked for one million more. I was on the conference call and told Trammell and Don Williams to walk away. "Tell them to go to hell" was how I put it. I had seen this happen before with my uncle in Paris and thought the deal would end in disaster, but I had only been there a week, so I didn't have much credibility at the time. Trammell was hungry to get the deal done, as were his partners, Holloway and Hawkes, who were being funded by Brandt's Bank in London, so they went ahead and paid the extra million. It would turn out to be a bad decision.

Trammell was an incredibly astute people person who grew his business by partnering with people he liked and allowing them to use his name and credit to set up their own businesses under his umbrella. He placed his trust in people, and this worked out really well with his regional partners in the United States. It made him a billionaire, so he expanded overseas, where, in 1973, he had about $400 million invested. As the CFO of Trammell Crow International, my job was to account and control the financial operations and costs of projects run by the international partners.

One of the first things I did was hire a CPA, David Jacobs, to be my controller of the international group, and a secretary, Pat. David would be responsible for assembling all of the numbers relative to each operation. Next, I started traveling. And I mean travel. In 1974, I logged 150,000 international miles traveling to Europe nine times, twice to Brazil, the New Hebrides, and a few other locations in between. I reported to Don Williams for every project, except for the Brussels International Trade Mart, where I reported to Trammell directly. I would go over to Brussels at least once every quarter for meetings and worked closely with their controller, Rene Verdickt, who prepared all of their books. Rene was Belgian, a CPA equivalent, fluent in several languages, and very competent and diligent in his work.

Trammell had developed extensive banking relationships and worked with some incredibly powerful people around the globe, including the Esteve family from Brazil, Armand Blaton (the Trade Mart general contractor), and the Cucurella family in Spain. The Cucurellas were a father-and-son team, and they had a joint venture with Trammell for Makro to build Walmart-like, cash-carry distribution centers in Madrid and Barcelona. On that project, I worked primarily with their CFO, Miguel, who I liked a great deal, but the problem was that he didn't speak English, and I didn't speak Spanish. I could understand some things. The Spanish word for "expenses" is "gastos," and I still remember that to this day. Other details proved to be incredibly challenging, so sometimes Miguel would have to pantomime the expenses to me. He was a short and wiry guy, and I couldn't help but laugh at some of his gyrations. It was challenging, and it took several trips to Spain over nine months to go through their books so I could understand the operation, but we got the job done, and had fun doing it.

On one of those trips to Spain, I was waiting in a long line at the airport to get through customs when I heard the gentleman behind me speaking on his large mobile phone in English. I assumed that he was an American, so I made a comment and we started talking. His name was Duane Bellmore and he was the President of the Spanish National

Railway. He was a really tall guy who used to race cars at Watkins Glen, New York. His wife was a Spanish psychic by the name of Maria Jesús, whose clients included top officials and economists in the Spanish government, as well as the prime minister. We would frequently meet for dinner during my trips to Madrid, and I got to know them both very well. One time, Maria Jesús took me to meet her psychic for a reading. I didn't go in with very high expectations, but the psychic proceeded to tell me that I was named after my great-grandfather, which is true. She went on to explain that he was my guardian angel and protecting me. She didn't know anything about me or my family, so I immediately became intrigued. It was an incredibly weird situation, and one that I never forgot. I certainly have been very lucky during my life, and I hope that my guardian angel continues to watch over me.

Trammell may have been very successful in the United States, but I quickly discovered that he was in business with a cast of characters overseas, the most outrageous being two brothers in Paris and Geneva, Larry and Glen Isaacson. I knew there was going to be trouble when I showed up at the Geneva office asking to see the books for the European operation, and there weren't any. These two guys were having a ridiculously good time on Trammell's dime. They had large apartments in Paris and Geneva, were flying around on the company's King Air, and throwing wild parties, all charged to Trammell. It was a zoo. They were completely out of control and spending money all over the place, with absolutely no oversight or discipline. It was truly a wild scene.

First, I told the brothers that they were under new restraints on expenses and use of the King Air. They wouldn't be using the plane for any more skiing holidays, and the three-day-long parties in Paris had also come to an end. They tried to complain to Trammell, but both Trammell and Don Williams backed everything I did. Next, I had to hire a forensic accounting firm to create the books for the European operation for the previous two years, and reconcile the bank accounts, which had never been done. That took a year and a half to accomplish. We even found a $100,000 check that should have been deposited months earlier, just sitting in a desk in the Geneva office. The European operation was that disorganized.

Paris wasn't the only location where I encountered problems. Trammell had a regional partner in Australia handling his operations in the South Pacific. Don Russell had been Trammell's tennis coach in Dallas. Russell was on the pro tour for a while before he became a coach at SMU. He was born in Australia, and apparently that's why he got the job to be responsible for the South Pacific, New Zealand, and Australia operations. Although Russell would later make considerable money in Southern California, in 1973 he was not a competent real estate developer. He didn't have a clue what he was doing when he bought 425 acres of land for a new hotel in Fiji. Along the shoreline in Nandi, there is a mangrove-type plant called taraire that you must remove if you want clear access to a beach. What Russell didn't know was that in Fiji, close to 90 percent of the land is owned by the Native Land Trust Board, and you need their permission to remove taraire. He bought the land without permission to remove the plant, so no beach was possible and no hotel on the island would be successful without a beach. Eventually, the land was sold without any hotel ever being built.

Russell got himself into another bind in the New Hebrides. He had purchased a large amount of land in the capital city of Port Vila and began building the Intercontinental Hotel. It was a big hotel with 225 rooms, but problems surfaced immediately. The kitchen equipment that was ordered didn't meet the local electrical specifications. Instead of 230 volts and 50 Hz, the equipment was the U.S. standard of 120 volts and 60 Hz. That meant everything had to be completely rewired

COMING INTO MY OWN

at a significant cost. However, there was an even bigger problem—there was no way to get enough people to the island to fill the hotel. Neither the airlines nor the ships in the area had that kind of capacity. It would be many years before the island had the tourist capacity to support the hotel.

The Intercontinental Hotel wasn't Trammell's only business in the New Hebrides. He had also purchased 10,500 acres for a cattle and timber operation. The ranch was being run by an Australian general manager who had hired a bunch of cute twentysomethings to do all the work in the large ranch house. While not as bad as the European operation, the ranch manager was also having a great time at Trammell's expense. As a country boy from New Jersey, I knew absolutely nothing about the economics of cattle and timber.

When I was on the island, I'd frequently go to an excellent French restaurant in Port Vila for coconut crab, which was a massive and god-awful ugly land crab that lived up in the trees. The crab was unusual, but the dish was absolutely delicious. They would sauté it in garlic and butter, and I would sit there for forty-five minutes trying to get every single piece of crabmeat out of the shell. During my visits, I used to chat with the hostess, a beautiful Polynesian woman named Dominique. When I told her what I was doing there, she said to me, "I have a friend you should meet."

That friend was Peter Yunghanns. He was a very wealthy Australian lawyer, investor, and polo player who owned a vineyard in Australia called Katnook that produced high-quality wine. Peter was also a partner with Elders, IXL, a major Australian conglomerate. On the island of Efate where Trammell's hotel and ranch were located, Peter owned the slaughterhouse. So, when I met with Peter at the restaurant, I made him a deal. "I'll buy the drinks, and you educate me on cattle operations." We hit it off, and while he drank copiously, I learned all about cow/calf units and the economics of raising cattle in the process.

Trammell became a billionaire because he cultivated excellent partners, but he also made some horrible mistakes. The partnership network built on trust worked for him in the United States, but it didn't always work overseas because he didn't have as much direct and regular contact with those partners. Had he been in closer proximity to partners like the brothers in Paris, he would have quickly realized that they were taking serious advantage of him. However, problems like that didn't become known until I went over there to take a closer look at what was going on. It became apparent to me that if you don't set up systems to monitor operations up front, you're going to lose a hell of a lot of money. Still, Trammell was flush. He was considered almost too big to fail, but he was starting to put that theory to the test.

It was 1975. A year had passed since Trammell had signed the Madrid deal, and it was no surprise to me when that deal turned out to be a disaster. Holloway and Hawkes were not successful in getting proper planning permission, and they had no presales for any space in the building, so the decision was made to sell the property. So, what do you do with the $9 million in debt that was used to buy the property?

It was left to me and the in-house attorney for Brandt's Bank, Peter Farren, to sort it all out, and propose who would pay for what. Peter had been with Linklaters and Paines at the time, which was the largest law firm in the U.K. He left to become the in-house counsel for Brandt's Bank. The negotiations got off to a rocky start and the first time we spoke on the phone was not a pleasant experience. Peter thought it was Trammell's fault that the deal had gone south. I took exception to that because the operating partners were the bank's clients, Holloway and Hawkes. They were the ones who sold Trammell a bill of goods. They were also the ones who recommended we pay the extra one million at closing. Peter and I had competing interests, and our relationship immediately became contentious. There were a lot of people involved in that deal, and a lot of moving parts, so things got complicated. And I had to sort it all out while traveling around the globe, trying to establish financial control over each of Trammell's deals.

For a while, it didn't look like anything was going to get solved, but things calmed down between Peter and me, and we realized that the land was probably only worth a couple of million dollars. We finally reached an agreement about who would pay what. I took the deal to Trammell and Don Williams while Peter brought it to Holloway and Hawkes and the bank. It was approved by everyone, and finally, after eighteen months of negotiations, the mess that was the Madrid Azca deal had been resolved.

I happened to be at a board meeting for the International Trade Mart in Brussels when the settlement documents were completed. I changed my flight to Dallas, so that I'd have a layover at Heathrow Airport in London. At 10:30 a.m. Peter Farren picked me up, and we went to the TWA Ambassador Club at Heathrow. After eighteen months of haggling, it was the first time Peter and I had ever met face-to-face. We signed the documents and then got on the phone in the Ambassador Club kitchen to transfer a couple of million dollars around to pay everyone off. The women who worked there must have thought we were nuts, but by 11:30 a.m., it was done. My flight home wasn't for another three hours, so the two of us proceeded to get royally drunk on Bloody Marys and congratulate ourselves on a job well done. Little did I know, that was the beginning of a lifelong friendship.

7

I'LL KNOW WHERE I'M GOING WHEN I GET THERE

WHEN I FIRST ARRIVED IN DALLAS, Trammell's nephew, Michael Crow, and Trammell's attorney, Dan Miller, took me around the city to jump-start my social life. We'd go out to hockey games, restaurants, and bars around town. I was having a lot of fun, but I could never truly settle in or have any real relationships because I was never home long enough.

I'd be in Dallas for a week and then fly to Europe for seven to ten days. Then I'd fly back to Dallas for another week before leaving again to fly off somewhere else, like Brazil. The most taxing trips were to the South Pacific. Getting there was often a two-day journey. I had to fly from Dallas to Los Angeles, and then to Fiji, where I'd get a day room in a hotel for six hours before getting on a small prop plane (because they didn't have jets at the time) to make the final five-hundred-mile trip to Efate, New Hebrides. I'd be there for a week and then make the journey back to Dallas. This went on for a couple of years. My life was chaotic.

I was living in a state of perpetual jet lag. I may have been physically present, but mentally, it often felt like I was in a different time zone.

Since I would travel to the same cities regularly, I'd slip into routines. I'd find spots to eat and have friends in each city. I slowly became a part of little micro-communities around the globe. When in Spain, I grew close with Duane Bellmore and Maria Jesús. I'd stay at the Hotel Amigo in Brussels, a very nice hotel and close to the Trade Mart. Trammell's local partner was Dick Palmer, an American with two young daughters who lived out in the country. His wife, Sally, was a chef-level cook, and they'd invite me over to dinner and to stay at their home whenever I was in town. It was an awful lot of fun to be around them because I didn't feel like I was away from home. When in Brussels, I would also hang out with Guy Sibret, the Regional Sales Manager for ITT WorldCom, whom I met when I mentored him upon his joining the company back in 1970. Guy was single and had great contacts all over the Benelux countries. His apartment had a large outdoor deck for wonderful wine parties, which I thoroughly enjoyed.

Throughout my career, I made great friends with fascinating people who proved to have tremendous resources. I was a C-level squash player, and when I lived in New York, I played with three guys every Saturday. One of those guys was Michael Gough, who at the time was a bodyguard/driver for the Australian Ambassador to the United Nations. Mike's beautiful wife, Mavis, was from Fiji, and she was the one who arranged for me to meet with some of the tribal leaders on the Native Land Trust Board. This is how I learned about the regulations for removing the taraire plants when Trammell and Don Russell wanted to build the hotel in Suva, Fiji. I was ignorant about the local rules and customs but was able to ask questions and gain insight that I would not have been able to easily acquire had it not been for my contacts back in New York.

It was at one of those parties in New York thrown by my friend John Capozzi from American Airlines where I struck up a conversation with his secretary's brother, Saul, who just so happened to be a general in the Israeli tank corps—he was part of the Israeli attempt to capture the Golan Heights from the Syrians during the Six-Day War. We talked for three hours, and he told me some amazing stories. At the end of the night, he said to give him a call if I could ever make it to Israel. Time passed, and I never took him up on the offer, but about a year and a half after I started working for Trammell, I found myself in Belgium and very much in need of a vacation. I was supposed to fly home to Dallas only to fly back to Belgium ten days later. I had yet to take any time off, so I decided to call the general. I told him, "Last we spoke, you were nice enough to extend an offer for me to visit. I'm in Belgium now and have eight days off. I'd love to come to see you if you're available."

"Great!" Saul said without hesitation. "Let me know your flight information."

I booked my flight and landed in Israel at midnight. He was there to pick me up, and he walked me through customs and immigration. The next day, we made a brief stop for his bodyguard to pick up a new sidearm before he took us to the battleground in the Golan Heights. The Syrians had the high ground, and Saul showed us where they had their pillboxes set up so they could snipe at the farmers in the valley below. I also saw where the Israeli tanks had to be pulled up a steep slope by armored bulldozers. After being there and seeing it all in person, I could not believe that Israel was able to take the Golan Heights. In another area, the Israelis had built defensive fortified U-shaped bunkers that were protected on three sides. The Israeli tanks could drive right into the bunker, but the turret would still be above the barrier and could swivel 360 degrees. While Saul was taking me on a tour of the battlefield, the sound of gunshots scared the hell out of me. For a moment, I thought we were being shelled. Saul laughed. It was his bodyguard testing out his new Beretta nearby. My relief was short-lived when I realized that the Syrians still knew where we were and could shell us.

The next day, I got to swim in the Dead Sea, which was so salty that when I was floating, the water only came up to my armpits. One night, I stayed over in the kibbutz where Saul grew up. I got to eat in the mess hall, and he gave me a tour of all the bunkers where the residents could hide if they got shelled by the Syrians or Palestinians. I was especially impressed by the fish-farming ponds for growing tilapia. We later visited the Wailing Wall and toured the grounds of the nearby Al Aqsa mosque, though we weren't allowed to go inside because we were not Muslim. We also toured the bazaar on the West Bank and took in all the stimulating sights and smells—especially the spices. It was an incredible week, and I had a great time, but I had to go back to work, which meant more travel.

Living in a state of perpetual jet lag had its challenges, but I was still very much in my element because I was stimulated by what I was doing and who I was doing it with. This was exactly what I thought I'd be doing when I graduated from the University of Michigan and took the job at Touche Ross. I have to give credit to my controller, David Jacobs, and my secretary, Pat, back in Dallas because, when I was gone, the things that needed to get done got done. I was in regular contact with Don Williams while on the road, but having worked for Podmolik, I knew not to call them at all hours of the night.

It wasn't just the travel and the people that I enjoyed. I was learning a lot and challenging myself in ways that I had not before. I had never done currency hedging. Trammell's income stream was in dollars, but he was borrowing in different currencies, so the exchange rate fluctuations could be substantial. He needed to make sure that he could fix the exchange rate cost by hedging and avoid the unknown cost of exchange rate fluctuations. I was learning about warehousing in Germany, Italy, Belgium, and Brazil and about the hotel business in the South Pacific and timber and cattle in the New Hebrides. There were so many different things going on all over the world that there was never a dull moment. I was in my thirties, excited about what I was doing, and I had great stamina. There was even talk of Trammell developing in Singapore, Hong Kong, New Caledonia, and Australia, which would have been great fun. However, I started to see cracks in Trammell's business model and knew this job wouldn't last forever.

Whenever I would land in the New Hebrides, I was immediately met by both the construction manager at the Intercontinental Hotel and the ranch manager. The hotel construction manager was knee-deep in problems and always had questions he'd been sitting on, which he'd ask me the moment I arrived. Many of these were operating questions that should have been directed to Don Russell, but Don was not there, and usually did not have answers, so they became my responsibility to address. My confidence in the project wasn't high to begin with since they were building a massive 225-room hotel without any way to transport sufficient guests to rent those rooms.

Trammell's financial problems were finally coming to a head for a couple of different reasons. Gerald Ford was president at the time, and with the economy in recession, the real estate business was tough. Prime rates increased from 6 percent in January 1973 to 12 percent in August 1974, making it almost impossible to turn a profit because we were paying so much in interest. That was compounded with the damage Trammell's partners were doing overseas. He was at his lowest and needed help from them, but some were reluctant to sell their projects and provide necessary cash to him. Several lawsuits followed, and since Trammell had insufficient cash to cover the debt service on many projects, he was on the edge of bankruptcy. If he had filed for bankruptcy, institutions like Citibank, Chase Manhattan, and Continental Bank would have had serious problems. Pulling himself out of the hole would be no easy task.

With all the partners and operating entities Trammell had all over the world, things were complicated. He owed a significant amount of money—over $500 million—so he hired Kenneth Leventhal & Company to help him work out all of the claims and the various payments to the banks. For the international projects, I was tasked with supplying the accountants all of the financial information on each investment. What Leventhal did was create a massive chart with Trammell in the middle and clusters all around for each operating partner and the banks to which they owed money. The interrelationships and cross collateralizations were a gigantic and chaotic mess with two hundred crisscrossing lines going in every direction. It was painful to look at, but that's what Trammell had to work himself out of to avoid bankruptcy. Trammell stayed on the periphery while Don Williams, Bob Glaze, and the accountants came up with a plan that would allow him to recover. I could tell that Trammell was under a lot of pressure, but even though he was facing bankruptcy, he was more upset that many of his partners, who he helped get started in business, nurtured, and allowed to do business on his credit, would not support him.

After taking a closer look, Trammell and Don Williams decided to close up shop in Italy, Belgium, Paris, Geneva, and the New Hebrides. The only projects that would remain open were the Trade Mart in Brussels and the warehouses in Germany and Brazil. That was it. There would be no additional expansion anywhere else, and with no growth, there was no need to have a CFO in charge of international operations. I sat down with Don Williams and came up with thirty-six issues that needed to be addressed to close up the international operation, and it was agreed that I would do that for them. When I was done, it was understood that I would be out of a job.

It took almost a year and a half to complete those thirty-six items, after which I knew that I would need to find a new place to work. I was tired of walking into situations and finding out that someone else had screwed them up. It was even more frustrating when those people didn't want to listen to me or take my recommendations. I thought, *Since I'm so damn smart, why not go out on my own and do it for myself?* If I screwed up, at least it would be my screwup. And even at thirty-six, I still felt like I had something to prove after getting thrown out of Rutgers. I never reconciled with that, and it made me feel like I was perpetually behind the eight ball and struggling to catch up.

While essentially working my way out of a job with Trammell, I started talking with David Jacobs and Trammell's tax attorney, Don Walker, about starting a company that would offer advisory services for foreigners looking to invest in United States real estate. Then on Tax Day, April 15, 1977, I officially left Trammell Crow and started International Investment Advisors (IIA, Inc.) with David and Don. I had no partnership interest from my time at Trammell Crow, and I didn't have a paycheck coming in, but I was living pretty well. I had saved up about $70,000, and that would have to be enough until the company became profitable.

At first, we set up the office in my condo, and I started making phone calls to the contacts in my Rolodex. Every pitch started the same way. "This is Fred Brodsky, formerly of the Trammell Crow Company and now of International Investment Advisors."

Those first few days were humbling. I did not get the kind of response I expected. Even those people whose support I thought I could count on would ask, "This is who from where?" I learned very quickly that it was one thing to be CFO of Trammell Crow International, and it was something very different to be out on my own with nothing. The vast majority of people I had interfaced with over the previous couple of years had little interest in doing business with me because I was unknown, untested, and had no track record. The rejection was terrible, and the telephone bill was even worse. Sixty days after leaving Trammell Crow, I received a phone bill for $1,200. At first, Don and David agreed to split it three ways, but that commitment proved to be too steep for them, and they chose to drop out of our venture instead, leaving me on my own. The financial pressure made me nervous, and I started to second-guess myself, but I knew that if I didn't believe in myself, I would never get anyone else to believe in me, so I kept going.

I got some help from Don Youngs, who was a friend of mine and the local managing partner at the headhunting firm Spencer Stuart and Associates. They had an office in Bryan Tower, and he had some extra space, so he rented me a tiny secretarial office with an even smaller desk and room for only one chair. I had enough money to hire a secretary, Janine, and then I started prospecting for business.

It's funny how business relationships evolve. Once I went out on my own, none of the institutions I had positive relationships with wanted to risk working with me, but then I got a call from Peter Farren, who was very aggressive when we were first tasked with working out the specifics of the Madrid deal for our respective bosses. A lot had changed over the eighteen months since we had resolved the deal, and Peter proved to be one of my biggest supporters when I started International Investment Advisors. He was now working at Linklaters and Paynes in London, and when I was in town recruiting investors, he introduced me to Susan, who was the lead manager of the reception desk for the firm. He even allowed his secretary, Amanda, to make appointments for me in London. Henri Lazarski, another attorney and a colleague of Peter in Paris, helped with introductions.

During our eighteen-month battle over the Madrid deal, Peter would complain to his wife, Vicky, about this unreasonable guy named Brodsky whom he had to deal with. On one of my trips to London, he thought Vicky and I should finally meet, so we all went out to dinner at the Dorchester Hotel. Afterward, Peter asked his wife, "Don't you see what a terrible guy he is?"

She told him, "I've never met anyone more like you in my entire life."

We became so close that I started staying at their home during my trips to London. And Peter wasn't the only one who helped me. I also got a call from Pat Gibbons, Bill Fishman's former assistant at ARA. Pat had left ARA and gone to work for Sam and Philip Barshop, who started La Quinta Motor Inns. Pat was the Executive Vice President at the time and came to me to help him finance a La Quinta location in Atlanta, Georgia. I got a small financing fee of $20,000, which wasn't very much, but I needed it, and it came at just the right time to help me stay afloat.

Not having a paycheck was scary, especially when my very limited cash started to quickly dwindle. Attempting to extend my independent business life, I solicited contacts to help others with personal financial planning, as I had done previously for friends. Don Youngs introduced me to Emma Lee Doyle, a noted sex therapist in Dallas. I helped her organize her investments and create an investment strategy for her and her two daughters. Lee was very pleased with the result and introduced me to one of her clients, for whom I did the same work on an hourly basis. The small income extended my survival until I got a break.

About nine months after leaving Trammell Crow, I received a call from Rene Verdickt, the former controller at the Trade Mart in Brussels. He had since left the Trade Mart and started working for Paul Calluy, who represented a group of Belgian investors who wanted to buy properties in the United States. In Europe, there was a very high personal tax rate, and the rate in Belgium was especially high, so a lot of business was done in cash that was not declared as income. It was that "black money" that Calluy was looking to invest in the Sun Belt, of which Texas was a part. The Trade Mart was Trammell's largest project, so Rene and I had spent a lot of time together. He had always been very responsive to all of my questions, was very competent, and we developed an excellent working relationship. It made sense to keep doing business together.

My work with Trammell was mostly hard construction. I knew little about land investment, so when I was approached by Calluy and the Belgians, I went to Russ Chaney, Executive Vice President of Hank Dickerson & Company, a broker in Dallas, who I had met previously. I told him that I wanted to establish a relationship with his company because I had some investors who were looking at land. He assigned me two brokers—Terry Gwin and Charlie Adams. Both were brand new to the business. Terry had just left his job as a sales manager at IBM, and he probably knew as little as I did about land investment and development.

It was around this time when I developed a relationship with Bill Kramer, who was the personal attorney for notable Texas businessman and sports mogul Lamar Hunt. Every Friday when I was in Dallas, Lamar, Kramer, some people from his office, and I would pile into a Suburban and go to this backyard rib place. We'd pick up our own drinks, pickles, and sauerkraut, and literally go eat in this guy's backyard. Butcher paper covered the picnic tables, and you ordered racks of BBQ ribs by the pound. Those ribs were so good that we had to keep coming back every week. Kramer would be instrumental in achieving my first income purchase, but first I focused on closing a land deal to consummate my business relationship with the Belgians.

Terry Gwin and I identified a potential property for the Belgian investors in Plano, Texas, owned by Ward and Stuart Hunt. They were asking for $11,000 an acre. I visited the property, and I liked it. I told Terry, "Put in an offer for $10,000. Let's see if we can get the land for something less than what they're asking for."

A few days later, Terry called me up. "I need to talk to you. Can you meet me at Bent Tree Country Club?"

"Can't you just tell me over the phone?"

"No. It has to be done in person."

That didn't sound good. I drove up to Bent Tree, got there first, and waited in the lobby. When Terry arrived, he sat down and told me, "I got a counter."

"Great! What is it?"

"Twelve thousand an acre."

It took a moment for that to sink in, and then I thought I heard him wrong. "They were asking for eleven, we offered ten, and they came back with twelve?"

"Yup."

We both sat in stunned silence for a moment. "Is that how this is supposed to work?" I asked him.

"I have absolutely no idea how any of this works, Fred. This is my first time doing this."

"Go offer him eleven."

That's what he did, and we ended up buying the property for $11,000 an acre, but that proved to be quite the learning experience. We were dealing with two consummate professionals, and a father-and-son team to boot, who had been there and done that. Terry and I can laugh about that experience now, and we often do, but I learned to know who you're dealing with and know the facts. If we knew that the property was not fairly valued at $11,000 an acre, we'd have something to leverage with, but we didn't. After that, I made sure I knew every single detail about a property I was interested in, including the development costs of competing properties nearby.

I established a 50/50 joint venture with the Belgian investors named Spring Creek Investments, which was named after the street where we purchased our first property, but I had more ideas for future investments. Lamar Hunt had recently developed Lakeway World of Tennis Resort on Lake Travis, which was located in the hills outside of Austin. He had sold two hundred of the 220 condos he had built, which meant that there were still twenty available that I could market to the Belgians. I made a deal to buy all twenty condos at a discount, and Lamar would personally guarantee an 8 percent return for five years.

When Rene, Paul, his brother-in-law Herman Kools, and twelve more investors flew five thousand miles from Belgium to Dallas to see the condos, I had to figure out how to get everyone to the site. I was familiar with King Air airplanes because that was the plane Trammell had in Europe, so I chartered three of them and put five people in each plane. The pilots were nervous because we were really testing the length of the Lakeway Airport runway for this type of airplane and weight, but it all worked out perfectly. When we landed, a caravan of Suburbans was waiting to take everyone to the sales office. We entertained the investors, had lunch, toured the World of Tennis, showed them the condos, and flew back to Dallas. Everyone agreed to participate, and they all paid cash. We had attorneys draw up contracts to purchase the twenty units, four of which I kept for myself using my commission on the deal as the source of funds. The $2 million deal was done in forty-eight hours. That was the beginning of what would become a very profitable relationship with Paul Calluy.

I was learning on the go. I never stopped to think about what I knew or didn't know about the business. I had complete tunnel vision and focused only on what I had to do to get the company up and running. There was no plan, other than to not screw it all up. I was in survival mode, but that wasn't difficult for me. Throughout my life, if I had money, I enjoyed spending it, but if I didn't have money, or I was concerned about my financial situation, I didn't spend it. Survival mode also meant curtailing my social activities, but ironically, my social life was about to take an unexpected and life-changing turn.

Since I still lived in Dallas, I kept in touch with some of my former colleagues at Trammell Crow. One Friday evening, I popped into Dan Miller's office at Bryan Tower to see if he wanted to go for a drink. He told me, "I'm meeting a friend after work, but you can come along if you want."

"Yeah. No problem."

Dan didn't tell me that the person he was meeting was a woman he was dating, and that he planned to end their relationship that night, so he could marry someone else. Darla Chick was one of Dan's girlfriends at the time, and she joined us at a restaurant called Elans for drinks. I sat there while Dan and Darla had this intense conversation, complete with histrionics, though some involved deny that it was anything but cordial. Maybe they remember it correctly because the three of us were getting along well enough to all go out to eat at a nearby Spanish restaurant owned by a friend of mine. After the restaurant closed around 11:00, my friend brought out a bottle of Carlos Primera Spanish brandy, which the four of us consumed in celebration of Dan's upcoming nuptials.

When we finally called it a night, I drove Darla back to her car at Elans and I asked to see her again. She agreed, but I was leaving the next day for Europe, so I told her that I would give her a call when I got back into town. I later found out that Darla had written my name down on a pad beside her bed, so she would remember who I was if I called.

My Grandmother, Celia

My Mom and Dad at their wedding

Me as a baby (circa 1941)

With my first rescue dog, Skippy, on the stoop of our Woodbridge home

My Bar Mitzvah at Adath Israel Synogogue in Woodbridge, New Jersey (1953)

My first car, a 1956 Ford convertible with a Continental Kit

Uncle Walter at his home in Paris

Vince Caminiti relaxing on 'My Way'

With my mom, partying in Dallas

Darla and me at our wedding (December 20, 1985)

Celebrating my birthday with Peter Farren in Dallas

Trimaran 'My Way'

Terry and Susan Gwin aboard 'My Way'

Mom on the deck at our Fairhaven house (2004)

*Celebrating my 60th birthday with Mom
and my brother, Greg, at our Dallas house (2000)*

Celebrating Rosh Hashanah with Darla, my Mom,
sister-in-law, Ching, and Greg in Santa Cruz, CA (2003)

One of the rescue lions in his quarantine cage,
San Juan de Aragon Zoo in Mexico City (1994)

One of three rescue lions in his new home
at Texas Exotic Feline Foundation in Boyd, Texas (1995)

In Paris (2010)

Christmas in Dallas (2010)

Maria, Darla, and me on a Regent cruise (2010)

Darla and me, Gus and Sadie at our home in Dallas (2010)

The Farren family at goddaughter Jessica's wedding in Chalgrove, England (2015)

Enjoying a round of golf with godson Ben Farren

Ben and Peter Farren and me (2015)

8

THE DALLAS
REAL ESTATE BOOM

I T WAS A VERY COLD DECEMBER NIGHT in 1971 when I was returning home to New York City from dinner at my mom's apartment
in Stamford, Connecticut, with a bag full of food. I arrived at Grand
Central Station to find that all of the taxis were on strike. I walked across
42nd Street to 2nd Avenue, in front of the UN building, to catch a bus to
my apartment on 83rd and 1st. As I waited, I could hear a kitten meow
on the far side of the street. Second Avenue is wide, so I could only see
a small blur moving back and forth. That meowing continued for more
than fifteen minutes. It was freezing, and I was grateful to have a warm
coat, but I felt sorry for the poor animal that was stuck out in the cold,
so I ran across the street, scooped up a tiny kitten, and went back to wait
for the bus. When it finally arrived, the driver told me that I couldn't
bring a kitten on board, so I stuffed her in my bag and got on anyway.

The kitten was ugly, sick, and scruffy, so I gave her milk, cleaned
her up, and put her into the bathroom for the night. A friend of mine
who was a vet at the New York Animal Hospital came over the next

morning to examine her and could tell right away that she had ane-
mia and a respiratory infection. "You have two choices," he told me.
"You can either put her down or take three months to nurse her back
to health." I nursed her back to health, and she turned out to be a very
strange but loving cat, and I named her Nightmare.

A few years later, when Gretchen and I split before I moved to
Dallas, I inherited her eighteen-pound cat, Munchkin. I flew to Dallas
with both cats in a carrier under the seat in front of me. Those first few
weeks, I stayed at the Sheraton while my apartment was being reno-
vated. While I was at work for Trammell Crow at his office across the
street in Bryan Tower, the cats would always get out when the maids
came to clean the room. They told me how they had to recruit the bell-
boys to wrangle them. When I moved into the apartment, my neighbors
looked after the cats when I traveled, but once I started dating Darla,
she would come over to look after them, and do her laundry because
she didn't have a washer or dryer at her apartment. That's when we
started to see more of each other.

Our relationship progressed slowly and a bit sporadically. I was
still traveling a couple of times a month, but Darla did get a chance to
meet my mother not long after we started dating. They took an instant
liking to each other. When my stepfather George retired and sold his
bicycle business, my mom tried to hustle my brother and me into finding her the best deal on a new place to live. Greg was living in Hawaii,
and I was in Dallas, but she knew some people in San Antonio, so that
was enough to get her to make the move from Connecticut to Texas. I
bought George and her a town house in San Antonio, and we'd usually
go down there every Mother's Day, Thanksgiving, and Jewish holiday.

Around the Fourth of July 1979, Walter and Maria traveled to the
United States from Majorca, dropped their three kids off at camp in
Maine, and met the family at Lakeway near Austin where I still owned

the condos from the Lamar Hunt deal. Walter hadn't changed one bit. He kept working into his eighties, but the following year, he was traveling to the Canton Trade Fair in China when he had a heart attack and died on the airplane. My mother and I flew to Majorca for the funeral. I'm glad that Darla got to spend some time with my uncle before he passed away.

Meanwhile, the Dallas real estate market was booming. I started to have a substantial cash flow, and that marked the end of "survival mode." By 1980, we had completed more than $100 million in transactions. I moved the company out of the office in Spencer Stuart and Associates, and into our own office on Central Expressway. I would handle the administration, buy, rezone, develop, and sell the properties, while Calluy would supply the money. Spring Creek Investments (SCI) was established as a 50 percent-50 percent joint venture and our business was land investment and development. SCI would buy the land and put in the infrastructure for single-family lots financed by Belgian investors. We'd hold those lots as inventory, and when the demand for single-family lots reached the area where we had properties, we'd sell the lots and return around 20 percent to our investors. They were ecstatic!

We were constantly busy, and it was always an adventure. One group of three investors came to town during one of the worst ice storms in the history of Dallas. They didn't care about the weather, they just wanted to see the land they had purchased in Plano, so we all piled into my Lincoln Continental. The trip was only twelve miles, but it took us two hours because we were sliding all over the road. Kids actually ice-skated by us on the street. We finally arrived at the property. It was farmland that had yet to be put into lots, but they still got out of the car and walked around. All three of them had huge smiles on their faces when they returned. On the drive back, my car skidded off the road and got stuck in a ditch. I had to walk to the nearest farmhouse and convince the farmer to tow us out with his tractor. Even that couldn't dampen the investors' spirits.

In 1981, I moved out of the condo and purchased a home on Grand Oaks off Hillcrest Road. I may have had a house, but I didn't have many dishes or glasses, so when I invited guests over for dinner, Darla always had to supply her china. Slowly, she started moving her things over to the house from her apartment. Darla was becoming a bigger and bigger part of my life, and when Calluy hosted a strategy session in Europe, he invited her to join me.

Calluy was married to the daughter of the president of the diamond exchange in Antwerp and living incredibly well. He chartered planes wherever he went, had a ski chalet in Gstaad, Switzerland, a collection of twelve-cylinder cars, and a home filled with antiques. He lived a lavish lifestyle and was spending a lot of money. Whenever we went out to dinner, it was common for the bill to be between $200 and $500 per person, so it was no surprise when he sent Darla and me two first-class tickets to London. When we landed, we were personally escorted off the plane and to a private jet that flew us to Antwerp, Belgium. When we arrived, we all had dinner in Antwerp, piled into three cars, and drove to Paris at 100 miles per hour. Calluy had rented a gorgeous estate on the outskirts of Paris for about ten of us, including Rene Verdickt, his wife, Anita, and his sister and brother-in-law, Herman Kools. The next morning, suffering jet lag, Darla had a bit of a meltdown when she wasn't able to get her hair dryer to work in the European outlets, but we were eventually able to get out and see the sights. That night, Calluy took everyone to Lasserre in Paris, a truly beautiful restaurant. Darla ordered everything she knew that was "French," including Coquilles Saint-Jacques, tournedos, and profiteroles for dessert. Each guest had an individual server and the wines kept coming during the entire meal. Lasserre was exceptional, including the elevator entry and opening roof. It was an incredible, knockout experience.

Life was good, and business was even better. Things were moving so fast that we were able to buy and then sell some properties on the same day for a considerable profit. In March 1981, I purchased 125 acres in Plano, Texas, for $1.25 million and sold it the same day for $1.5 million and made a quarter of a million dollars. The following year, I bought 11.25 acres in Mesquite, Texas, for $610,000 and sold it the same day for $660,000, then another 202 acres in Fort Worth for $6.1 million that I sold the same day for $8 million.

We were so successful that Calluy started making promises to his investors that I wasn't comfortable keeping. He invited me to Antwerp to meet with potential investors. He introduced me as his United States partner and talked about all that we accomplished. And then he told the investors that he could continue delivering these same returns. Calluy was pointing to me as the guy who would guarantee those returns, and that's when I got upset. Real estate is a very cyclical business and trends usually occur in seven-year cycles. I wasn't comfortable making promises of future returns and that what had been accomplished or realized would continue indefinitely. I flat out told him that he couldn't make those kinds of promises. This disagreement led to more than one serious argument. I told him that I would not put my name on anything that said the return would continue or be better than 20 percent, but Calluy continued to make these commitments and that was the beginning of the end of our partnership.

In 1983, Calluy and I decided to split the joint venture, and we reached a mutual agreement about how to divvy up the properties. Mike Burris, who I had hired as a property manager and then as VP of Finance, took advantage of the schism and went to work for Calluy. Calluy and Burris thought they could do what I did better, and without having to share 50 percent of the profit with me, they continued to buy properties together under the SCI name. Mike became the head of their office in Dallas, but a couple of years later, SCI and Burris each went bankrupt.

I moved into a new office in the Transwestern building at Park Central and started buying properties on my own and developing my own accounts. It had been four years since I'd left Trammell Crow, but I finally had the experience and the track record to develop a client base in India, Pakistan, and Kenya. A couple of the Belgian investors from my deals with Calluy, who I had gotten to know well, decided to continue to invest with me. They turned out to be great clients, and I'm still in business with one of those families, forty years later. When it came to European clients, I had a leg up on the competition because I spoke passable French and understood a little Spanish and German. Some people went so far as to say I was as much European as I was American because I was aware of the cultural differences given all the time I had spent overseas.

It was my due diligence more than anything else that got me ahead, and I got really good at identifying patterns of growth and anticipating where development would take place. When dealing with land, the greatest increase in value is just before it's ready to be developed. That means when the property has available water, sewer, zoning, or planning permission, access to highways, and an increasing demand. According to the Land Residual Value Theory, land is only as valuable as the economic return created after deducting development costs. If utilities aren't available at a reasonable cost, the land will not be sold to a developer, only to another land investor, and your return will not be as great. I purchased a sixty-nine-acre property in 1984 that I still own because the city never made the utilities available. When utilities finally become available in the next couple of years, the price will go from the original purchase price of $700 per acre to the current value of $10,000 to $40,000 per acre, or more, and we will eventually earn a significant internal rate of return (IRR), but only after almost forty years.

Before buying any piece of property, I always made sure to do my homework, and often that involved spending hours up in a helicopter scouting out land to purchase. Texas is the bottom of a prehistoric lake, and looking down from above, I could see which areas were prone to flooding. If you can understand what areas will flood, the cost to mitigate that flooding, and the quality of soils, it can give you a competitive advantage. Landis Aerial was a company in Dallas that prepared aerial photographs and compiled them in a book that had the photo of the land on the left and the zoning information on the right. I'd refer to that book when I was up in the helicopter, and once I'd targeted an area I wanted to buy, I'd ask Terry Gwin to track down the owners. Sometimes it took months to talk to an owner who may or may not want to sell the land, but most of the time, we were successful. One of my favorite deals was when I bought 275 acres in Hickory Hill for $2.75 million and sold it one year later for $12.5 million, making over $9 million in profit. I bought it for $10,000 an acre and sold it to Terry for $1 per foot, or $43,560 per acre. He then resold it a few months later for $3 per foot. It was wild.

It wasn't just the way I found and developed land that was different at that time, but also how I structured the deals. There were a lot of wheelers and dealers in Texas, but I went out of my way to keep things as fair and as simple as possible. After seeing all the problems that Trammell Crow had with syndications and investors, I tried to avoid creating the same problems that he was forced to endure. Trammell had hired some incredibly smart people who had experience in how to structure deals. When things worked perfectly, there wasn't a problem, but the financial arrangements, cross-collateralization, and credit enhancements were so complicated that it made it next to impossible to resolve any problems that developed easily, inexpensively, and quickly. What I did instead was put up 20 percent of the equity and have the investor put up 80 percent. They received no interest or preferred return, and I would cover all of the general overhead. When we sold, we first received our equity, then we'd share any profits 50/50. If my client didn't make money, I didn't make money.

I also made sure I only had one investor per deal. We never put more than one asset into any joint venture. Even if we had a series of deals with the same client, it would always be a separate joint venture. At one point, I had thirty different bank accounts, one for each venture, because I wasn't commingling funds. If I were working with a family, then we'd designate one person for me to interface with. That eliminated any potential confusion and saved me a lot of time. I wanted to do things my way because if something didn't work, the simple structure made it easier for me to fix the problem. I was fortunate not to have many problems to fix—not yet, at least.

I also continued doing business with some of my old friends. Pat Gibbons had left La Quinta and started his own motel company called Texian. I joined two other investors, one of whom was the son of a Texas senator, to put up $100,000 each. Pat owned the majority and was the president, while I owned about 16 percent. He immediately started doing deals and building motels. The first three were great—they were well designed, well built, and well located.

Pat felt that he was in competition with his former bosses, the Barshop brothers, and he wanted to build more Texian units than La Quinta had, so he started to get aggressive. He cut a deal with a savings and loan for a lot of money, which we all agreed to fund and guarantee on a joint basis. That meant we were not only liable for our share; we were liable for the total amount that was borrowed.

Pat started buying locations. Once he'd spent over $20 million, I looked at the numbers and had serious concerns about what was going on. It was one thing to guarantee one or two million dollars, and it's another thing to guarantee $10 or $20 million. With three units up and running, we shouldn't have had to guarantee 100 percent of all our new debt, which was what Pat was doing as an incentive to get financing. The lenders weren't seeing the residual value in the existing motels, and that concerned me. It didn't quite pass the smell test. Pat and the other investors were incredibly optimistic, but I was the only one who had some money in the bank, so I didn't need the risk.

"I have a deal for you," I told Pat. "My business is going great. I want to concentrate on that. If you give me my original $100,000 investment back and get me off all of the liability on the $20 million investment, I'll do that deal."

"You're crazy," he said. "We have all this equity and all these operating units. The first few are doing well, making money, and are certainly worth more than what they cost."

"Pat, that's my deal. I really want to focus on my own business. Take advantage of that and just get me my investment back, but make sure to get me off all the liability."

"I'll go to the other guys and the lender and see if they'll agree."

It took three months, but Pat came back to me and said, "I got it done. Here are the documents. Give up your interest, and I'll write you a check for $100,000. The bank will sign off and release you from all liability."

We did the deal, and I got out. A few years later, Texian and the other investors all declared bankruptcy.

•••

Money was a scorecard, not the end goal. Darla and I may have gone to some lavish parties in the area, but my lifestyle remained relatively the same as it was before I started making money. To me, financial success meant that my basic needs were met and that I could live the lifestyle I wanted to live. Anything more was style and ego. I didn't spend a lot of money on clothes. I think my mom gave me the best watch I ever owned for college graduation, and I still own clothes that are over twenty years old. I wasn't frivolous with my money, and I was able to live on very little when I didn't have it. That didn't mean that I couldn't appreciate the finer things— I learned that from Walter. I'd travel to Europe with Darla, and after I finalized the Hickory Hill deal, I paid $100,000 for two used cars—a Rolls Royce and a twelve-cylinder Jaguar—but I wasn't living an extravagant lifestyle by any means, especially in comparison to the other Dallas real estate developers. I did, however, make one extravagant purchase.

When I first arrived in Dallas in the early 1970s, I got PADI certified to scuba dive, and through scuba diving, I met Buford and Geri Beach. Buford was the head of aviation for Southland Corporation. They had a fleet of a dozen airplanes, and he was the chief pilot. Geri owned a small retail store. One night, Darla and I were over at their house for dinner when Buford pulled out the plans for the sixty-foot trimaran he was designing. He was looking forward to using the boat when he retired in four years and was currently working on the plans with a naval architect named Ed Horstman, who had designed a line of Tri-Star multihulls. The yacht was going to cost Buford about $750,000.

After the second bottle of wine, I asked him, "How much could we save if we built two at the same time?"

It was a very expensive question. Buford looked into it and, a few days later, told me that we could probably shave a quarter-million dollars off the construction cost of each boat. I had never thought of owning a yacht before that dinner, but it sounded like a good idea at the time. I loved learning to sail on Toms River when I was a kid. After I graduated from the scuba class, four couples chartered a trimaran called *Misty Law* in the Caribbean, and I'd thoroughly enjoyed those two weeks. Darla and I talked it over and decided to go for it. The idea would be to charter the boat in the Caribbean to help offset the operating cost, and use it ourselves a few times a year when it wasn't being chartered.

Buford negotiated the contract to build the two boats with John Casanova, who had built several Horstman designs. Casanova was also a phenomenal sailor and an expert when it came to storm conditions and multihulls. We refined the designs, and since my boat was being built for charter, it had a different interior configuration than Buford's. I had five guest beds, room for three crew, a one-hundred-bottle wine cellar, sixty-seven cubic feet of refrigeration, a double stove, and two dive compressors that were capable of filling twelve tanks in thirty minutes. The mast would be sixty-seven feet tall and carry two thousand feet of sail.

During construction, I dragged Darla to the Miami International Boat Show, so I could research all of the decisions we needed to make. Those days were long—probably twelve hours each. One evening in the hotel elevator, I turned to Darla and said, "We're going to have a really exciting day tomorrow." Her eyes lit up, thinking we were going to the beach or do some sightseeing, but then I told her, "We're going to look at engines!" She deflated, but that was my idea of an exciting day.

Everyone kept telling me what I could and couldn't do when it came to design. For example, I wanted seven feet of headroom in the main salon but did not want to increase the windage of the boat. After doing some research, I realized that I could countersink the floor by eight inches and get my seven feet of headroom. I eventually found a way to accomplish all of my objectives. With the design in place, we just needed a name, and I fittingly decided to call her *My Way*.

The hulls were built first in Galveston and ferried over to Port Boli-var, Texas, where Buford had found a shed big enough for the boats to fit nose-to-nose and be assembled. That's where the final construction began in early 1982, and what followed was a two-year saga that ended with the assembly and installation of the single Perkins diesel engine in September 1984. The boat was then ready to sail to Derecktor Shipyard in Fort Lauderdale, which is still one of the highest quality boatyards in South Florida, so we could finish the interior. First, we had to get *My Way* in the water.

The launch was an exciting event. Darla and I arrived in Galveston the night before and took the ferry over to Port Bolivar in the morning. When we turned the corner on to the street where the shed was, they had already taken the massive steel doors off the shed and backed the boat out onto the road. It was the first time we had seen her from the side in its entirety, and she looked huge!

They had to jack up the boat and slide a massive twenty-two-wheel trailer underneath that they hooked up to a dump truck. The street by the shed was a two-lane dirt road, and there wasn't enough room for the trailer to turn, so they had to hook up a second truck, and have them both turn the trailer with *My Way* secured by lines. Even though the mast was lying flat on the deck, she was still extremely high. Once on the road, guys stood on the boat with poles to lift up the telephone lines, so the boat could pass underneath. Many local residents turned out for the event and followed us to the launching site.

When we arrived at the launch site and backed *My Way* partially into the water, four guys had to get into the water, myself included, and attach the eight-foot rudder. One dump truck was disengaged, and the second backed up slowly, so the rest of the boat could ease into the wa-ter. Once the water hit the stern, *My Way* started to slide off on her own, but fortunately, we already had lines attached to the deck. It wasn't picture-perfect, but the launch turned out fine, and there was a round of applause from everyone present. We were relieved to know that she floated and stayed dry inside!

Every boat needs to be christened to appease the god of the sea, Neptune, and it was that time for *My Way*. Darla climbed out on the bow with champagne bottle in hand and said, "Through lots of sweat, even a few tears, and lots of standing at the Florida boat show, this boat is being appropriately named for a song that begins, 'Concerns, I've had a few...' I christen this boat *MY WAY!*"

And with a crash, the bottle was broken. On September 7, 1984, *My Way* was official.

Captain Warwick Lowe and his wife, Barbara, took *My Way* on the three-week journey through the Gulf Intracoastal Waterway to Derecktor Shipyard in Fort Lauderdale where the electronics, interior, and plumbing were installed. One of my old New York friends, Michael Young, owned Hy-Drive in Australia, and he supplied all the hydraulics. The interior work took another seven months to complete, and I was getting invoices every week for about $10,000. By the time *My Way* was finished, she cost me $1.2 million. The experience was worth it because Derecktor's did a magnificent job on everything, especially the woodwork, right down to the matching grains on all the drawers and doors.

When Derecktor's said the boat was ready, Darla and I joined about thirty other people for what is called a sea trial to see how the ship performed on the water. We had all the people on board who worked on the electronics, screens, navigation, generator, engine, refrigeration, and sails, and all the construction guys, to make sure the equipment was calibrated correctly, and everything was operational. It was a rough day at sea, with some six-foot waves. Michael Young turned green, but I was in seventh heaven.

The boat had to return to Derecktor's for the final touches, and then it was ready to be provisioned for the trip to Saint Thomas, where it would be based. We would charter her for eighteen to twenty weeks a year, which was a lot for that type of boat, and it was an extremely successful charter boat until the industry deteriorated after Hurricane Hugo hit the Caribbean in 1989. When it wasn't being chartered, Darla and I would take trips with friends like the Gwins and the Caminitis three or four times a year. We sailed all over—up to Maine, down to Trinidad and Tobago. I kept that boat for eighteen years and she is still in successful charter service today.

Success to me wasn't just about buying things and improving my lifestyle; it also meant I had the freedom to pursue different projects and endeavors that I was passionate about. In 1983, I read a story in the *Dallas Morning News* about a young boy whose puppy had run away. The boy was heartbroken and wouldn't eat. He posted signs and checked the pound daily, but the dog never turned up.

What had happened was that the puppy had wandered into the next town, where it was found and brought to the shelter. The problem was that the dog didn't have tags, and nobody knew it was there, so after ten days, the dog was put down.

After doing my research, it became clear that the city had a huge problem with stray animals. At the time, the Humane Society was estimating that 178 pets went missing every day—and 65,000 animals went through Dallas's twenty-two shelters every year. Fewer than 10 percent of these animals were ever recovered by their owners. They either died of starvation, got hit by a car, or were destroyed in the shelters. Moreover, it was challenging politically to pass regulations that made it mandatory to neuter animals, which compounded the problem.

That boy's puppy didn't have to die, and neither did any of the pets who got lost in the shelter system. *Why not come up with a database linking all of the shelters where a pet could wander?* I thought. We'd provide a central phone number that owners of missing pets could call and learn which shelters were holding pets that met the same description as the lost pet. Even if someone found a pet without a tag, they could call the number and use the description of the pet to track down the owner. So long as shelters talked to each other, the hotline could be a central registry for all the shelters in the area.

I called Pat Loconto, my first boss at Touche Ross, who had since advanced to Director of Worldwide Consulting for Deloitte & Touche. He put me in touch with a software expert, and together we developed the idea that would become PETNET, a computerized lost-and-found system for pets in the Dallas area. We tracked all types of animals, but it was mostly used for dogs and cats. Today, databases like that are common, but back in 1983, they were unheard of.

The city loved the idea and agreed that the program would be operated by the Dallas Department of Health and Human Services, but they didn't have the $200,000 necessary to purchase the software, so we had to rely on donations. We were able to raise $100,000, and then Deloitte & Touche put up the remaining money to get the program running in 1985.

I was able to do the things I wanted to do, but Darla also had expectations of her own. Up to that point, most of the women I dated only stuck around for eighteen to twenty-four months before they realized I was serious about not getting married. Darla and I had been together for seven years. I had told her that I saw no reason to get married and that I did not want children. Even though she'd make an excellent mother, she accepted the idea of not having children, but she had been pushing for a commitment, and it was in the summer of 1985 that she finally gave me "the ultimatum." I told her that I needed some time to think about it, which I did. In September, a week before we were supposed to travel to

Europe for work, she told me, "If we aren't going to get married, you can go to Europe by yourself, and it will be a good time for me to move out."

As a confirmed bachelor, it took me three months of consideration before I came to the conclusion that I valued our relationship, and I did not want to lose her, so I decided to propose. I was forty-five years old, so I couldn't propose just any old way. Laurie and Dana were friends of ours who owned a flower shop. I told them that I wanted an old funeral wreath with dead flowers and for the card to read, "Here lies the single life of Darla Joyce Chick." I had a perverted sense of humor and thought this would be unique.

The night I proposed, Darla was hosting a dinner party at our house for her good friends Steve and Oliver, so I had Laurie and Dana deliver the wreath to the front porch before she arrived home. When Darla finally saw the wreath, she immediately called Steve and left him a scathing message because she thought he was playing a joke on her. "How could you joke about this? You know how important Fred is to me! We're at a critical moment."

After thinking about it for a while, Darla's next call was to my assistant, Karen Bryan. "Karen, did Fred send me flowers?"

"Um, I don't know. Do you want to ask him?"

When I got on the line and Darla asked if I had sent the flowers, I said, "What did the card say?"

"I didn't find a card but let me look again." She went to look, came back, and told me, "There was no card, but there was a ribbon." It turned out that Laurie and Dana had put the message on a ribbon that was tied to the wreath instead of on a card. "Fred, does this mean what I think it means?"

"We'll talk about it when I get home," I said.

We couldn't talk about it right away because of the dinner party. That night, I sat at the end of the table, didn't say anything, and quietly proceeded to get inebriated. The next day, Darla suggested that we get married at city hall, but I knew that she wanted a nice wedding, so that's what we decided to do, and it was the best decision of my life.

We started planning the wedding and then left for Europe together. While in Paris, we shopped for Darla's wedding dress at Chanel and Dior, but it was in a small shop called France Favor that she found the perfect dress. It took trying on a couple of them, and some people felt it was bad luck that I had seen her in her wedding dress before the ceremony, but we shared a special moment in that tiny little store. After Paris, we traveled to London, where I asked my friend Peter Farren to be my best man. We even changed the date so that two of Peter and Vicky's three children, Ben and Amy, could be in the wedding. By the time we were back home, we knew that we wanted to get married in our house, so we decided to have the wedding on a Friday night in December and then host our big company Christmas party the very next night.

Darla and I have always complemented each other exceptionally well. Being insular and single had made me myopic, and Darla has always been a great sounding board because she has better insight into people and some situations than I do. I'm incredibly direct, blunt, and politically incorrect, so whenever I'm writing or doing something that requires a sensitive touch, I always run it by Darla, who usually finds a better way for me to get my point across without upsetting people. Still, the transition from being a confirmed bachelor to getting married at the age of forty-five was significant. I didn't have much balance before I met Darla, but she has taught me about the importance of having a well-rounded life. After the wedding, I realized that, for most of my adult life, I had been selfish in a way, but that had all changed, and I had now evolved into someone who wanted to share everything with another person. Darla became part of who I am, and I couldn't be happier.

9

WHAT GOES UP
MUST COME DOWN

WHEN DARLA AND I FIRST STARTED GOING OUT, she would invite me up to the lake house her family owned on Lake Texoma to show off her waterskiing skills. Over the years, I got pretty good at waterskiing, but I was never as good as Darla.

We were up on Lake Texoma on a regular basis, and in 1980, I saw a great opportunity in the town of Pottsboro, Texas, to purchase and develop 180 acres of land. The problem was that it belonged to sixty heirs of an estate, and it took me three and a half years to convince the family to sell. Texoma did not have any upscale condo communities, so I began developing what would become Summer Cove, but it was a complicated deal. I had to get permission from the county and town to run a four-inch sewer line for two miles along the highway to a waste treatment plant.

Pottsboro was a small town where the mechanic was also the mayor. When I'd go there to negotiate the zoning, he would show up to city council meetings in his T-shirt with a pack of cigarettes rolled up in his sleeve (just like I used to do as a kid) and spit chewing tobacco into a Styrofoam cup. I was eventually able to build fifty-two condos, and they looked great. By 1984, I had forty reservations, but by the time construction was completed in 1985, only one of those sold. That was the beginning of the end of my dramatic financial performance.

At the time, I had $10 million cash in the bank and thought I was bulletproof, but I failed to see what was coming. In 1985, I purchased $33.6 million worth of properties, most for my own account, but I started to see that the market was too inflated. The success and returns I had experienced were not going to last, so I stopped buying property that year. It was a year before everyone else stopped, but it wasn't soon enough. The economy had been booming. Everyone was making a ridiculous amount of money. Real estate developers had boats, mansions, planes, private chefs, and some even sponsored race car teams. Then, it all came to a screeching halt.

It was excess, greed, and really dumb government policy that caused the market to crash, about eighteen months after I got married. At the peak of the real estate boom in 1985 and 1986, Congress, in its infinite stupidity, reduced the down payment requirement on a home loan to virtually zero, so you didn't need any cash equity to buy a house. Corrupt appraisers would overvalue assets, so the banks could loan more money than the house or building was worth. The savings and loans (S&Ls) were allowed to participate in joint ventures, but they were essentially unregulated, so they accepted loans and earned up-front fees while lending money on long-term assets that didn't have the value they were being loaned against. If it were a $10 million development deal, the S&Ls and banks could loan more and take the excess in front-end fees, loan costs, and facilitate developer overborrowing. There was no economic justification for this at all. Banks were taking huge 5 and 10 percent fees, so they were getting significant up-front profits on a $10 million loan, and the developer was walking away with cash in his pocket after buying the assets. The underwriters had no reason to fairly value the development as the profit was made on the front end. When the excessive loans started to fail, S&Ls were going bankrupt, so the government, in another brilliant move, set up the Resolution Trust Corporation (RTC) to take over the bad assets of the S&Ls. They hired guys and paid them a ridiculous amount of money to liquidate the real estate owned (REO) assets. Instead of trying to work out the problem loan with the borrower, the government discounted and packaged the underperforming loans so syndicators could buy them and securitize the loan packages. These were all underperforming assets, but they included a lot of land. Because developers borrowed so much money against the land, there was no economic reality left for anything to be built on that land. And since land is only worth what you can put on it (minus construction costs necessary to generate an economic return), the overvaluation of land destroyed any potential economic return. The government had billions and billions of dollars of REO assets worth less than the debt. Many of the appraisers hired to evaluate these assets were corrupt and taking payoffs. With so many REO assets on the market, getting a fair, balanced, and appropriate valuation was extremely difficult. The government started selling REO assets at ten cents on the dollar owed. They were even financing that ten cents at below market interest rates.

I may have had $10 million in the bank, but I also had personal contingent liabilities of $42 million. I was sitting there and had all of this great land that I had borrowed against, but there was no way in hell that I could sell that land at any reasonable price if I were competing with the government owned REOs. I had just gone into business with a major Australian conglomerate, Elders IXL, which I was introduced to through Peter Yunghanns, my Australian contact from my days with

Trammell Crow. Elders committed $500 million for a U.S. joint venture, but even that was put on hold when the real estate market cratered. I also owed them money from my share of the liability on a great piece of land in Fort Worth (our first project together) since they were carrying my interest because I had no cash flow. When we mutually agreed that we wouldn't be able to develop that property because of the economy, I owed them $2.5 million for my share of the loss, so I deeded them part of the property I owned on the east side of the highway by the DFW Airport. They would later go on to sell that property for a lot of money, but at the time, I didn't have a choice.

Nobody was going to pay me the fair value on any of my property when the government was packaging and selling land at deep discounts to syndicators. It wasn't long before I ran out of cash, and when I couldn't make my payments on my debt, everyone came after me for what I owed all at the same time. In five years, I had gone from being worth over $70 million on paper to being underwater by $42 million, not including penalties and interest on the $42 million debt.

It wasn't just me who suffered. A lot of my friends in the real estate business declared bankruptcy. They were the ones who went out and bought airplanes and mega-mansions. Some got divorced because they had wives who had gotten used to spending $5,000 a month at Neiman Marcus. The government can't foreclose on your home. You can use home equity to start over, which was why a lot of real estate investors and developers went out and bought huge mansions.

I didn't want to go that route. After I left Trammell Crow and set up my own company, I knew that it was on me if I made mistakes or lost money. If I created the problem, I needed to find a solution. I had started to anticipate what was coming, but not soon enough. You have to understand the environment around you, and how it affects your business, whatever that business may be. My current financial problems were a result of my naivety, so it was my failure, and I had to deal with it. Bankruptcy was a cop-out, in my opinion. Maybe that thinking had something to do with my ego, but I saw bankruptcy as an unacceptable tactic. I needed to work my way through my financial problems, and I had to do it alone as I could not finance any professional support.

My strategy was to stay afloat while holding on to the 130 acres near the north entrance of the Dallas-Fort Worth Airport in Grapevine, Texas, until I could get fair value for that property. The problem was that there was a severe discrepancy between what the property was really worth and what the appraisers were saying it was worth, so I had to ride it out. I kept that property away from creditors while trying to use everything else I owned to satisfy my debts.

Since I didn't have any money coming in, I even tried to see if I could work for someone else and earn a salary. My first call was to my good friend Pierre Benoit, the former mayor of Ottawa, Canada, who had moved to Dallas and became a real estate developer. He wanted to hire me as an analyst, but once he started asking about my computer skills and how well I could develop spreadsheets, it was immediately clear that I wasn't qualified. He wasn't the only one who turned me down. As I began making calls, people would ask if I knew anything about all of these software programs that were in vogue at the time. I didn't know squat then, and I'm still not computer literate. I wanted to go to work, but nobody would hire me, so I couldn't get a job.

By 1990, I was hanging off the edge of the cliff by two fingers and quickly losing my grip, but I did have one fail-safe plan. Before Darla and I got married, we both signed a prenuptial agreement to make sure that she was protected if my high-risk business went south. According to that agreement, I owed her $5 million, so I decided to deed her my one-third interest in a thirty-five-acre piece of property on the Texas

Toll Road in satisfaction of that liability, and to ensure that the property was protected from creditors if things got even worse.

It was around this time when I got a call from Maria, Uncle Walter's widow. "I need a favor," she said.

"Okay."

"Our son Peter is in school in France and has to get a summer job or an internship, but he hasn't been able to find anything. I would like to send him to work as an intern for you."

The timing wasn't great, but I knew that it was something I had to do. After what Walter had done for me when I got thrown out of Rutgers, of course I said "yes."

Darla and I hadn't seen Peter since Walter's funeral ten years earlier and had no idea what he would look like. Darla thought he might have purple hair, but that was not the case at all. He was polite, interested in the business, and a lot of fun to have around. Maria had insisted that Peter listen to me, not cause problems, and do whatever I asked under "penalty of death," so he arrived ready to work, but the work I had to offer him was limited.

The real estate market was in such disarray that we were still trying to lease the Summer Cove condos, even five years later. I didn't have any cash to keep paying anyone else, so we put Peter to work as our on-site salesperson and moved him into the model unit. He did a good job, but after a couple of months, he went home and finished up school in France. He would later move to Boston to get his MBA at my alma mater, Northeastern, before returning to Majorca, where he married his high school sweetheart, Victoria, and had three kids.

Despite Peter's efforts, I was getting taken to the cleaners on the Summer Cove property. I was making debt service payments on the $5 million I had borrowed for the land and development costs, including the costs of maintaining the property. The bank asked me to put up some additional cash, and we agreed to $500,000. That's where my naivety came into play because what I should have done was offer to put up the $500,000 and have them get me off the personal liability. I don't know if they would have done that as a quid pro quo, but I wasn't smart enough to ask, so at the end of the day, I sold the condos for $2 million in bulk and had to pay the interest, penalties, and property taxes, which, when it all added up, meant that I lost $5.5 million. That was a big hit.

Meanwhile, Darla and I were living day-to-day. We bought the Dallas house on Royal Lane back in 1984, so our priority was making those mortgage payments. We were doing very little else, and there was almost no money coming in. Once I stopped doing business with Calluy, I had started my own construction company, and always had an engineer do a development feasibility study on every piece of property we purchased. When I stopped buying property, I dissolved the construction company. By 1990, I had let fifteen employees go. I was able to keep five, along with James Toal, my partner in Fort Worth. In 1992, we closed both offices and had our bookkeeper work out of our house, which wasn't as common as it is today, especially in Dallas. Not long after, we had to let the bookkeeper go, too, and Darla ended up doing all of the business accounting and administration.

When you can't pay off your debt, the bank and their lawyers can call you in to examine your assets. What made this process exponentially more difficult was that the government assumed that everyone who owed money and could not service their debt was a crook. Luckily, I had never gotten greedy, skimmed, or lured into making deals that I didn't think were sound business decisions. Some of the Belgian investors were connected with the Antwerp Diamond Exchange at a very high level. They had offered to pay me in diamonds and keep the money offshore. I did think about it, but ultimately turned down the offer and declared everything I earned to the U.S. Government and paid my taxes. All investment cash received went into joint venture bank accounts, so it was all accounted for and there was an easy-to-follow audit trail. Every venture was a separate deal with a separate bank account, so the funds were never commingled. Nothing was done under the table because I felt that life was too short to spend it looking over my shoulder. I never made any money unless my clients did, and if my clients lost money, so did I. Luckily, I had gotten out of the Texian deal just in time. Not only did the other three investors declare bankruptcy, but the bank tried to come after me as well. In the end, those good, aboveboard business decisions were what saved me, but that didn't stop the banks from coming after me and their attorneys calling me a crook.

I wasn't hiding anything, so I would sit through lender's interrogations with my attorney Marshall Dooley, an ex-Marine who was about six feet two. I went in there with my passport, federal tax returns, and bank statements, willing to be up front about everything. Almost immediately, they accused me of hiding money. They suggested that I had bought jewelry and was hiding it in a vault somewhere out of the country. My blood started to boil because there was nothing criminal about my business, and I was doing everything I could to be honest with everyone in the room, but it didn't matter. It got so ugly that, at one point, Marshall had to physically restrain me from leaping over the table and cold-cocking the unreasonably aggressive lead attorney.

I considered myself an honest person with a set of principles. There were many people in Dallas real estate, friends of ours, who were going to jail for some relatively incidental stuff like falsifying financial statements, but I never did any of that. There is nothing that I'm ashamed or embarrassed about, which was why I got so incredibly upset with the accusations being made against me. We were seriously struggling both in business and personally, so to be accused of being dishonest by bank attorneys was the low point in my life. And things weren't getting any easier.

Despite having no reliable cash flow, I still tried to make deals. I had signed a contract to buy a 182-acre piece of property north of Fort Worth, but it hadn't closed yet. Ross Perot Jr. wanted that property because it was a critical piece of land that he needed for his Alliance Airport project. Perot came in and offered a million dollars more than what the seller and I had agreed upon, so the seller reneged on the contract he had with me. When that happened in 1993, I hired Roger Goldberg, the head litigation partner at the firm Durant & Mankoff, and sued the seller for "specific performance," which was the remedy specified in the contract.

In any contract, you put up consideration. It was customary at the time to put up a check for a sum, in this case $5,000, that was held (and not cashed) as consideration for the contract. Perot, through the seller, got his lawyers to argue in court that the uncashed check was insufficient consideration and the contract was an option, therefore cancellable at any time. The trial lasted for an entire week, and the jury ruled that the contract was enforceable and affirmed my right to buy the property. I won, but the seller, supported by Perot, decided to appeal. I didn't have the money to pay extensive legal fees, so I reached a written agreement with Roger Goldberg. I would pay fees, but no overtime expenses, third-party expenses at cost with no markup, copying expenses at a nickel a page—the terms went on and on, and it was all detailed in a letter agreed to and signed by Goldberg.

The appellate court reversed the ruling of the lower court and said that there was no consideration for the contract, which meant the seller could terminate the contract at any time. Now, it was my turn to appeal. Durant & Mankoff kept assuring me that the contract they prepared was legally binding. The case went all the way to the Texas Supreme

Court, which affirmed the appellate court ruling that it was only an option and not a contract. Perot won. The reason being that I had not paid out any cash in consideration to the seller. If I had paid even $50 to the seller in consideration, I would have had the right to the property, but since no was cash was exchanged, it was an option. That case became a notable one for real estate in the state of Texas, and Perot went on to build the Alliance Airport, which is now a sizeable commercial airport and development.

When I lost, Durant & Mankoff sent me an invoice for $6,500 in expenses that they said I had underpaid throughout the nine-month ordeal. These were expenses that I wasn't obligated to pay, per my deal with Roger Goldberg. My jaw dropped when I saw that invoice. *You just cost me a couple of million dollars, and now you're coming after me for $6,500 in expenses?* I went back and audited all of the expenses and realized that they actually owed me money because they had overcharged me by $9,500. They had charged me for secretarial overtime, parking tickets, express mail, excessive copying costs, and all the things that Roger and I had agreed to in writing that they wouldn't charge me for. The problem was that Roger Goldberg had died right after the trial, and Ron Mankoff and the law firm came after me for those expenses. They sued me, and Ron's son, Jeff Mankoff, served as their legal counsel in court.

I was on the ropes and had no cash to hire another lawyer, so I decided to represent myself. Before I had to appear in court, my clients in England wanted to meet in London, so they sent me a plane ticket. I went to the SMU Law Library and got a book titled *The First Trial: Where Do I Sit? What Do I Say?* and another book on the legal proceedings in the state of Texas. I read both of those books and took extensive notes on the flight to London and back.

Mankoff wanted a jury trial, so when I got to court, Jeff Mankoff and his team of two lawyers and a law clerk were on one side. I was on the other side with all of my books, which were filled with color-coded sticky notes, and Darla rooting for me from behind. They would file a bunch of motions in the afternoon, and then Darla and I would be up until three in the morning, poring over these books to learn the jargon, so we could understand what was happening, and then file our own responses the following morning.

At the trial, when it was my turn to call witnesses, I tried to introduce into evidence the letter signed by Roger Goldberg. I put Ron Mankoff on the stand. I asked him, "Mr. Mankoff, is this letter on your firm's stationery?"

"Yes."

"Do you admit that this letter is from your firm?"

"No." Mankoff flat out lied.

"Is this Roger Goldberg's signature?"

"I don't know."

Mankoff was sitting on the stand and knew it was Roger's signature and written on his letterhead. He knew that I had made a deal all along, but he would never admit to any of it. Every time I tried to question him about the letter, Jeff Mankoff immediately objected. The judge knew that I was representing myself, so she was patient with me. "Try again, Mr. Brodsky. Ask the question a different way."

"Excuse me, Your Honor," I said as I went back to my desk and combed through the books with the colored sticky notes to figure out how I could get the letter introduced as evidence. I even tried to get on the stand myself, and talk about the letter, but Jeff would always object. I never got the letter introduced as evidence, but Mankoff knew that it proved my case. After three days, they asked for a temporary adjournment. Ron Mankoff came to me and said, "We are willing to walk away."

"No way," I told him. I wanted the jury to rule on it. I couldn't get the letter into evidence, but I was able to get in my spreadsheet that showed what the firm charged and that they actually owed me $9,500. Ron Mankoff and the firm knew they were wrong, and I think they wanted to avoid being embarrassed.

Darla and I waited in the courthouse while the jury deliberated for about an hour and a half. We took our seats as the jury came back in and handed the judge the verdict. She read it to herself before turning to the Mankoff lawyers and asked, "Would you like to poll the jury?"

Darla and I had no clue what that meant, and had no idea what was going on, but all three of the Mankoff lawyers turned white. "Yes," Jeff Mankoff responded.

If you lose the verdict, you can ask for the jury to be polled and have them verbally acknowledge that they voted for the judgment. That's what happened, and the judge asked every juror, "Does Mr. Brodsky owe Durant & Mankoff any money?" Every single one of them said, "No."

Mankoff lost. I didn't pay them anything, including the $18,000 in legal fees they demanded, but I could never collect any of the money Mankoff owed me because, in my own ignorance, I never counterclaimed, so the jury was never asked if they felt Mankoff owed me any money. I may have won, but I still had only a superficial idea of what I was doing.

After the trial, I went up to the judge and asked, "How could I have introduced that letter into evidence?"

"You would have had to say that you saw Roger Goldberg sign something—a letter or a receipt—so that you could confirm that it was his signature on that letter. Without that, I wasn't able to authenticate it."

As Darla and I were walking out, we bumped into four jury members who asked us what was in the letter. When I showed it to them, one of the members told me, "I would have given you whatever you asked for."

That wasn't the end of it. I then hired a lawyer who specialized in legal malpractice who represented me on a contingency basis (meaning he would receive 40 percent of any settlement) and I sued Durant & Mankoff for legal malpractice because the original contract they drew up for me failed due to no consideration, a basic contract requirement. I think the trial was a serious embarrassment to Mankoff and the firm within the legal community, because they lost to me in court and because of the flimsy contract. That contract cost me a few million dollars, but I won the malpractice suit and was awarded $300,000, which I desperately needed.

That wasn't the only time I had to defend myself in court. The second time happened shortly after a bank foreclosed on my summer house in Lake Texoma. I had borrowed $150,000 to buy the house a few years earlier, but by the early nineties, I had no cash and couldn't pay the mortgage. They foreclosed for $75,000. That's what their appraiser said the house was worth, so under Texas law, they came after me for the difference between the foreclosed valuation and the amount I had borrowed.

It turned out that the president of the bank bought the house, which was interesting. Then, I looked at the form the appraiser filled out. The head of the firm had checked the box saying that he personally inspected the house himself. I knew most appraisers never inspected these houses themselves and almost always sent someone else from the office. They were doing so many foreclosures back then, so it seemed far-fetched that the head of the firm would personally inspect anything for $150,000.

The first thing I did was have my own appraisal done, and that report indicated that the house was worth $135,000, so I only owed $15,000 compared to the $75,000 that the bank was demanding.

When we got to court, I put the appraiser on the stand and asked him, "Is this an appraisal from your firm?"

"Yes," he said.

"Is this your signature on the form?"

"Yes."

"Did you personally conduct this appraisal?"

"No, I didn't."

"But you represented that you conducted this appraisal, so how did you arrive at this number?"

"We had someone from the office go by."

"What type of appraisal was it?"

"A drive-by."

"So, this guy didn't actually go inside and inspect the house?"

"No, he didn't."

After hearing that testimony, the court decided to go with my appraisal, which meant that I only had to pay the $15,000.

Between going to court and staying afloat, I was so focused on surviving that I wasn't able to keep up with all of my business ventures. Years earlier, I entered into a joint venture with two women to buy an apartment complex in Richardson, just north of Dallas, that they were responsible for managing. They were a little younger than I was, and had other properties, but they were high rollers who started putting their friends in the apartments, and they began selling drugs. One of the women's boyfriends would steal cars, and he turned the back of the property into a chop shop. I had no idea what was going on until I started getting calls in the middle of the night from some elderly tenants complaining about the air conditioning being broken. When I drove to the property and saw what was going on, the women promised to clean it up, but when nothing changed after three months, we agreed to sell the property and dissolve the joint venture. That was a headache that

I didn't need.

Everything was changing and life was starting to look completely different. With no more office or employees, we had to phase out our traditional Christmas party in 1993, and we decided to go out with a bang. We called it our "Bottoming Out Party" to celebrate what we hoped was the end of the real estate depression. We had a soup kitchen line. I printed up bumper stickers that read: "Oh, Lord, please let there be one more real estate boom, and I promise I won't piss it all away this time." We had the valet parkers put those stickers in everyone's car. A lot of people decided to come in costume. Terry Gwin came as a land broker, which meant that he dressed up as a bum with holes in his pants, and his wife, Susan, went as a leasing agent who was dressed to the nines since leasing agents were still making money.

The party might have been premature because we hadn't quite hit bottom yet. There were opportunities that I could not quite take advantage of, and one deal that imploded due to unusual circumstances. I had bought a great property in north Fort Worth and negotiated seller financing for twenty years. Without cash, I was not able to make the semiannual payments, so I entered into a joint venture with a fascinating British character named Bruce Owen, whom I met through friends of Peter Farren. Bruce was an extremely wealthy young man, a silver spoon baby who came from family money. He had his nanny from his childhood come in every morning and serve him freshly squeezed orange juice. In addition to his in-town estate, yacht, and the collection of Ferraris that he kept in an air-conditioned garage across from his London town house, he was a champion glider pilot despite being short, stocky, and afflicted with gout due to his extravagant lifestyle.

Bruce had come in on a home run of a property of 150 acres that I negotiated over many months. Once the joint venture agreement was signed, he visited us in Dallas and brought us a kilo of beluga caviar as a gift. Darla and I were leaving on an international trip in two days, so we didn't open up the caviar and share it with him as it would have spoiled while we were gone. He got so upset with us over not being served the caviar gift that he had provided that he hired a lawyer with the objective of removing me from our deal. His lawyer did not understand real estate or land and came up with all kinds of representations about the land in our joint venture, none of which were accurate, but served to cast doubts on my integrity and the value of our land. I had no money and wasn't funding my share of the liability and debt service, so Bruce could try to push me out of the JV. There was absolutely no reasoning with him, and this lawsuit dragged on for a year. I ended up paying some serious legal fees to a lawyer in Fort Worth. In the end, they forced me to sell the property for $6 million. I strongly objected because I knew the property was worth a lot more, and sure enough, six months later, the property sold for $30 million. Had he not insisted we sell, Bruce and I could have made $15 million each, instead of $3 million, and I could have easily paid off my remaining debt, but it didn't happen because I never offered to share the caviar he brought. A couple years later, Bruce had elective lap band surgery and died on the operating room table. The caviar story became a running joke with Peter Farren, but neither Darla nor I could think of anything else that would have changed Bruce Owen's attitude.

I don't have many true friends, but I received great support from the ones I did have. I had gotten to know Craig Hall when I called on him to sell some of my land in Plano a few years earlier. He was a well-known developer in the Dallas area—very smart and astute. When it came time for me to network and see what I might be able to do to generate some money, I gave him a call. He also owned a yacht, so during our conversation, my boat came up. I needed cash, so he agreed to loan me $300,000 against *My Way*. He also hired me as a consultant to look at some of his land holdings and do an evaluation of the development potential for those tracts. It wasn't much, but the loan and those small consulting fees for a few thousand dollars kept us afloat.

I had slowly been chipping away at our debt through sales and deeding properties to lenders in settlement. From 1986 to 1988, I sold $6 million. In 1989, I sold $16.5 million in six different transactions, and in 1990 I sold $8.7 million in four separate transactions, but none of this was going into my pocket, so money remained tight. By 1995, I still owed $5 million, and we were down to our last $10,000. Darla and I had a decision to make: either spend $5,000 on the mortgage or give it all to a bankruptcy attorney. For almost ten years, we never purchased anything we didn't need. We never missed a meal, but I was at the end of my rope. I had run out of options and resources, and it didn't look like I would be able to sell any more assets. I picked up the phone a couple of times to call the bankruptcy attorney. I had his number written down on a sticky note on my desk, but I never made that call. After much deliberation, we decided to pay the mortgage and keep our fingers crossed that something would happen. Then, exactly forty-five days later, something happened.

10

IN THE CLEAR

AFTER I PURCHASED THE LAND IN GRAPEVINE in the early 1980s, I gave the State of Texas sixteen acres free and clear, worth about $5 million, for the right of way to build SH (State Highway) 2499. The agreement was that I would give them the land, but they had to put the highway where I wanted it. So, I hired a land planner to go in, lay out the property, and work out all of the details to put the highway in the optimum location for me to develop on each side and create more value. There was a green belt to the north of the property, which was primarily floodland, but the area around it was slowly starting to develop.

That property turned out to be a great location to build a shopping mall, so I was approached by The Mills Group and began negotiating a deal to sell one hundred acres for what would hopefully become the Grapevine Mills Mall. It was a deal that would allow me to pay off the remainder of my debt and keep the remaining thirty-one acres, which I could then sell and use the proceeds as seed funding to start making money again. Mills was also looking at alternative sites, so they were in the catbird seat, and the negotiation became tortuous. It went on for months. They would send teams to negotiate in my home. There were a whole host of issues, mainly the price, access, and cross-access easements to perfect utility placement for the remaining thirty-one acres. I needed to protect the remainder of the property and create as much value as possible. On multiple occasions, I told them, "Okay, guys, we're not going to reach an agreement, so you should move on to another site." Just as often, they would get up and threaten to focus on another piece of property. Darla would be in the next room, listening to all of it unfold, and it was painful for her, but I had no choice but to push. If I didn't get enough money to pay everyone off, whoever I still owed money to would take the entire property, and I'd have nothing. I had to make enough to pay my taxes and settle with everyone I owed. That was my bottom line.

The negotiation was a roller-coaster ride, but after nine months, we finally got the deal done and closed on one hundred acres at $7 million. The next day I paid off the remaining $5 million I owed and also the mortgage on the house. After more than ten long years of lawsuits, depositions, and being called dishonest, the strategy I came up with was successful. We survived without ever declaring bankruptcy and were finally home free and clear of the entire $42 million of debt I had accumulated.

When you dig yourself out of a hole like that and recover, usually one of two things will happen: you'll go crazy with the money you think you have and spend it on frivolous things, or you'll realize that the experience was terrible and do everything in your power to ensure that it doesn't happen again. We had made enough on the land sale to continue being generous while living a comfortable lifestyle, so we chose the second option.

Those ten years were a significant imbalance in my life, and the only reason I survived and made it through was because of Darla's support. She never complained or tried to tell me, "This isn't what I signed up for." It was the opposite. She did whatever was necessary to help me survive, and that would not have happened without her in my life. Darla and I were closer than ever, but unfortunately, right when things were back on track, another significant loss occurred.

Twelve years earlier, after George passed away, my mother had moved into a retirement home. Even though she was already in Texas, she decided to be closer to Greg and his three boys, who all lived in Santa Cruz at the time. She wouldn't drive in the snow or ice, so she would be more comfortable in California. She may have been in her eighties, but she still loved to drive, though never at night, so I'd bought her an Oldsmobile Cutlass that was built like a tank. If she ever got into an accident, she would be fine because that car was made out of solid steel.

The retirement home in Santa Cruz was called Dominican Oaks, and it was a retirement community for priests and nuns. It took some convincing at first, but once she agreed, she moved there and fit right in. A little Jewish lady, who still had a Jewish-Russian accent, became best friends with a nun, Mary Jo, and had all the priests in love with her. She immediately made her presence known. She organized trips to Vegas, got the residents involved in line dancing, threw costume parties, and even appeared in an ad for the home on television. She had her favorite places around the city, including a restaurant on the Santa Cruz pier. Darla and I would fly out there and spend time with her, and we'd also get to see my brother. Then, on September 15, 1995, she passed away at the age of ninety-three. Right up until she passed away, she had a hearty appetite and was still driving her car.

After my mother passed away, my brother and I went our separate ways, though in truth, we had been going our separate ways since our father's death when I was fourteen. We've never had a great relationship, mainly because we have different values and different approaches to life. Greg went a completely different route and is much more metaphysical than I am. He's written a couple of books on neurolinguistic programming (NLP) and martial arts. He's a tai chi master who had his own dojo and was licensed to practice acupuncture in California. He was a highly paid consultant who earned $3,000 a day as an executive coach, but he never cared much about education, finances, or planning for the future. Other than him being my brother, we have little in common. He's been married twice and raised three boys, but I don't have any relationship with my nephews. I'm godfather to his oldest, but even when we visited my mother in Santa Cruz, we didn't get to spend any time with his kids.

•••

After my mother's passing, I took a deep breath and went back to work. I had paid everyone off, and more importantly, I could catch up on some of the things that I had personally wanted to do. I had my MBA from Michigan but had graduated in 1967. I'd realized that it had been a while since I upgraded my skill set, so in 1989, I signed up for a class called Owner/President Management (OPM) in the Harvard Executive Education Program. It required three weeks on the Harvard campus for three consecutive years, but after the first year, I no longer had the money to continue. I reapplied in 1998, and they accepted me, allowing me to come back to finish. I joined a group of one hundred business owners from all over the world, and we all stayed in the dorms for three weeks. The companies those people ran ranged from being worth a couple of million dollars to one that did over a billion dollars in annual sales. It was quite a diverse group. In addition to upgrading our management and computer skills, we even studied some cases that were written about the companies owned by some of the participants. We had the top professors at Harvard Business School teaching us, and it was intense. One weekend, I met Darla for an impromptu rendezvous in New York City, but as soon as I arrived at the hotel, I took a shower, jumped into bed, and fell asleep for twelve hours.

I graduated from the program in 1999 and developed a good core group of thirty friends from all over the world. That was the real benefit of the OPM program. We stayed in touch after graduation, and every year, we'd religiously plan a trip hosted by a participant in his or her home city. We've gone all over—Australia, China, Panama, Colombia, Dominican Republic, India, Canada, Switzerland, and various cities in the United States. We talk about what's going on and get seriously candid with our business, health, and even marital problems. They are an impressive group of people and a reliable support system. Everyone is spread out over the globe at this point, but I try to see OPM friends every opportunity we have. These relationships have withstood the test of time, and I relish them all, which is a big deal for someone like me who is not particularly gregarious.

It was fun to be able to do the things I wanted to do, but I was also reminded of how old I was getting, and that wasn't particularly fun. In 2000, we went to London for Ben Farren's graduation from the University of Cambridge. I didn't feel great, but I assumed that I was just tired. When we walked to the ceremony on Saturday, I had to stop because I had trouble breathing. After that happened a couple more times, we went to the ER, where I was told I had unstable angina. Against the doctors' orders, I checked myself out of the hospital and drove ninety minutes back to Peter's house but promised them that I would return to the hospital if it happened again. Sure enough, it happened again, and we went to a different ER and spent the entire night there. Because we were flying home that Monday, the doctor gave me an inhaler to relieve the symptoms. Before we flew back, I phoned my doctor in Dallas and made an appointment for as soon as I arrived. Darla and I had been up for two days, so once we got on the plane, we went right to sleep and were out the entire flight. I was a little short of breath a few times while walking through the airport, but we dropped our bags off at home and went straight to the hospital. The situation was much more serious than any of us had realized. My left anterior descending artery, the widow-maker, was 95 percent blocked, so they had to put in two stents.

I was lucky to have made it home—my grandfather must have been looking out for me that day. Coincidentally, Darla and I had already signed up to participate in another Harvard program called Odyssey, which focused on "what to do with the second half of your life." After taking the OPM course, I had been getting mailers, and that course piqued my interest. Suddenly, the course objectives had newfound importance.

The course was broken up into two parts—the first was a week-long session that I attended alone on the Harvard campus. I was back to staying in the dorms again. There were fifty of us in a class taught by Professor Shoshana Zuboff, a clinical psychologist. The day after we arrived, we had to pick a dyad partner, someone we didn't know anything about. You had to trust that person because the mutual agreement you made was that everything you shared would be private. Mike Day was my partner. He was a young man from England who had recently sold his business for a lot of money and didn't know what to do next. During the day, Shoshana put us through a series of exercises that forced us to focus on what was really important—family, money, religion, lifestyle, and free time. She would pick out any inconsistencies if we tried to manipulate the choices or weren't being completely honest. It got pretty intense and revealing, so by the end of the week, I walked away with newfound clarity about my value system and my priorities.

Everyone went home for three weeks with some assignments and reflected on what we had learned before returning with our significant other to the Black Point Inn in Maine. When we arrived, Shoshana approached Mike and me and asked if we would partner up with a third guy whose partner didn't return for the second session. It was a man suffering from macular degeneration who had to deal with going blind in addition to a slew of other concerns. We agreed. The addition had only a small effect on us but helped both the man and his wife a lot. Many of those in the group were dealing with some heavy issues, and there were a few emotional sessions that left people in tears.

During one exercise, the couples paired off and were given an easel and a set of different-colored crayons. We were then instructed to draw a picture of what our future would look like together. We had to do it as a team, but without speaking a word to each other. That proved to be interesting, but Darla and I worked very well together. One of the biggest revelations for Darla occurred when she drew herself walking next to me instead of following behind, meaning that we would be equal partners.

At the end of the program, I left realizing that there were various things that I was holding on to that were causing me stress and unnecessarily sapping my energy, focus, and resources. That's when I came up with a three-year plan to rid myself of those added burdens, and it started with the biggest one.

The market had stabilized, so I had been working a lot since getting back on my feet. I was able to sell additional properties and start new ventures, but that also came with some added baggage that was causing me a lot of stress. I was holding on to many of those properties, hoping that I could get more money for them, but the writing was on the wall, and it was becoming increasingly clear that it wasn't going to happen as quickly as I had hoped.

Darla and I sat down and asked ourselves what we might do differently if we had more money. The answer was essentially nothing. We had a boat, but we didn't buy fancy cars and didn't want an airplane or designer clothes. We didn't need a mansion with servants or jewelry. I had no interest in becoming a billionaire (assuming I could make that much) and making money just for the sake of making money didn't make any sense to me. So, what was I working for? Yes, I was a deal junkie, but I was also sixty years old and didn't want to run the risk of getting battered about the head and shoulders again like I did when the market crashed. Once I was confident that we could continue living comfortably, Darla and I decided that I would start to transition out of the business and into "retirement." Plus, Darla said she'd break my fingers if I signed a deal on another piece of property or created an unreasonable amount of debt.

We had already moved out of the office and into the house years earlier, so there was no big adjustment there or additional staff to consider. I would liquidate what I owned, and I wouldn't do any new deals, joint ventures, or investments where I was the general partner or managing partner. We then came up with a plan to manage the assets we had accumulated since 1995. I was conservative going into the market crash, and I was even more conservative after. So, if I don't know how I'm going to pay for something, we just don't buy it. What I did do was invest half in the stock market and equities. I needed professional management for that, but I made sure to split it between two individuals instead of having only one manager. Everything else—real estate, oil and gas, venture capital—I did myself, so a lot of my time immediately after retirement was spent trying to manage my financial resources. With all of that squared away, we could then turn our attention to the things we were passionate about.

11

THE ART OF GIVING BACK

I N FEBRUARY 1994, I read an article in the *Dallas Morning News* about five male lions in Mexico City that were going to be euthanized. They had been kept in quarantine cages for five years because there was no room at the zoo for them to be displayed. The San Juan de Aragon Zoo failed to use contraception, so these lions were all born into captivity. It was one of those things that I read about and immediately knew that I had to do something.

Darla and I talked that same day and came up with a course of action. The timing wasn't great because I was still underwater financially and didn't have any personal resources to utilize, but I had connections through the Dallas Zoo, so I got on the phone and started putting a team together to get these lions out of Mexico City and safely to the Texas Exotic Feline Foundation (TEFF) in Boyd, Texas.

We negotiated a deal with Gene Reitnauer at TEFF for the cost of constructing the enclosures where the lions would live. We would have to raise $60,000, and since the lions were going to be euthanized soon, they agreed to begin construction immediately. I had built up some goodwill with the Chairman of the Board of Republic Bank, and he agreed to set up an escrow account for donations. My old friend, Vinny Caminiti from American Airlines, had since been promoted to Senior VP of Sales, and he convinced operations to divert a DC-10 (a bigger plane so the cages would fit) to Mexico City when it came time to pick up the lions and transport them back to Dallas. Kathi Travers of the ASPCA, who had been responsible for shipping Siegfried & Roy's tigers around the country, arranged to get the transport cages for us from the Bronx Zoo. I also called Rich Bickerood, the Director of the Dallas Zoo, a retired Air Force pilot who happened to have grown up in my hometown of Woodbridge, New Jersey. Rich arranged for a Dallas Zoo vet to go down to Mexico City every month to check in on these lions. On his first visit, the vet determined that two of the lions were in such bad shape that they had to be euthanized, but the remaining three lions could be saved. That was our team. They didn't do it for any reward—everyone volunteered.

Vinny also arranged for American Airlines' PR agency, Temerlin McClain, to make announcements and put out press releases. We even gave the rescue effort a name—Operation Pride. This was 1994, so the project coincided with the release of *The Lion King*, and Temerlin Mc-Clain helped us organize an event at one of the theaters in Dallas. Even a local radio station did a happy-hour fundraiser. Once the word got out, the money started trickling in. We only had one or two big donations of over $1,000, so most were small donations of $2, $5, or $10. And we received a lot of those. People poured their hearts out for those three lions: Rocky, El Negro, and El Canelo.

There were so many causes out there where you would donate your money and never find out what happened, so we tried to do something different by creating a newsletter. We got the names and addresses of the people who donated off their checks and sent them a newsletter with updates about what was happening at each step. Each newsletter had a donation slip, and some people kept donating.

In November 1994, nine months after I first read the article, we were ready to go pick up the lions, but I had a feeling that getting those animals out of Mexico was going to be difficult. Even though we had filled out all of the documents, double-checked them with Kathi Travers and American Airlines, I didn't expect things to run smoothly.

I knew that Jim Wright, a former Texas congressman and Speaker of the House, had incredible contacts in Mexico City. Jim and I had been having lunch about once each quarter for several years in Fort Worth and I knew his executive assistant from other activities I had been involved in. We even continued our lunches during his treatment for mouth cancer and had gotten to know each other very well, so I called him up and told him what we were planning. I said, "If I run into a problem down there, I'll need some leverage."

He gave me a phone number. No name, just a number. "If you have any problem, just call this number. Tell them that we're friends, and they will take care of it."

The vet went down to Mexico City on Sunday to stabilize the three lions for the trip. Kathi Travers and a reporter from Channel 8 in Dallas followed soon after to oversee the process. Kathi had the transportation crates shipped from the Bronx Zoo to Mexico City ahead of time. Darla and I got there Monday afternoon and arrived at the zoo just as they had finished examining the lions for the flight back to Dallas, which was scheduled to leave at 9:00 a.m. on Tuesday morning. None of the Mexican authorities wanted to process the paperwork, so Kathi and Lisa from American Airlines Cargo went to the zoo at 6:00 a.m. Tuesday morning to make sure everything got done properly.

Darla and I got to the airport and boarded the DC-10 that American Airlines had diverted for the 9:00 a.m. flight. Darla had made lion-themed corsages for all the flight attendants and certificates for the rest of the passengers on the plane to commemorate the rescue trip. Everyone was excited. It was a carnival-like atmosphere, and Channel 8 filmed it all, but then someone from the ground crew came aboard to say that they couldn't load the crates with the lions on board the plane because the customs paperwork had not been completed and "necessary documents were missing." This was complete BS as Kathi and Lisa had both carefully checked that all paperwork had been properly completed and filed. I knew American was on a tight schedule, so I told the captain, "Give me ten minutes."

I raced off the airplane, found a phone, and called the number Jim Wright had given me. A woman answered, and I said, "Hi, this is Fred Brodsky. I'm a friend of Jim Wright. Here's the situation: we have these lions on the tarmac waiting to be loaded onto the airplane. American Airlines can't hold the plane, and we'll lose the opportunity to rescue these animals if we can't take off now."

"Thank you, Mr. Brodsky. I'll see what I can do." That was all she said.

I got back on the plane and waited. We were running out of time, and I didn't think we would make it, but then all of a sudden, the captain came up to me and said, "We're all set to go! The lions are being loaded onboard now." I let out a huge sigh of relief as they loaded the crates with the lions onboard the plane. There was applause, some people were crying, and we managed to take off without incident. I have no idea who that woman I spoke to was, and I have no idea what she did. Some questions are better left unanswered.

When we landed at DFW, there was a mass of people waiting for us at the gate and press from every local television station and newspaper and even CNN. The whole thing was a whirlwind—we never set out to create such hoopla. The important thing was that the lions made it safely to TEFF. El Negro lived there for six more years, but Rocky and El Canelo went on to live long happy lives.

That experience stayed with me for a long time—not just what we were able to accomplish, but how great it made us feel. Operation Pride was more rewarding than almost any professional success I had achieved. On a visit to TEFF, I even got my hand lick from El Canelo. It was awesome to be licked by a lion!

Fast-forward to 2000. I was finally out of debt, and Darla and I were living comfortable lives. We spent our money on travel, and other than boating, we didn't have any expensive habits. We had the luxury to do what we wanted, but what does it all even mean when you don't have children? Is there a purpose to all of the sorrow, angst, and joy we all experience? The answer depends on what's important to you. For me, what made me happy and gave me the most satisfaction was helping others, be it people, animals, or a worthy cause, so that's where I chose to focus my attention post-retirement.

Craig Hall had stuck his neck out for me only a few years earlier when I was on the ropes, but he wasn't the only one. Countless people helped me along the way, and I never forgot about those at the Travelli Foundation who, back in 1967, had given me the $2,000 I needed to finish up my MBA at the University of Michigan. So, we donated $2.5 million to my alma mater, Northeastern University, where I received my BSBA degree. Over more than fifteen years, I served as an Overseer and spent eleven years as a Trustee of Northeastern University. Inspired by my "Ugly American" situation, we funded the first Trustee Professorship in Global Business, and contributed funds for the International Business Program. I had observed that American businesspeople were not as well versed as they needed to be to effectively compete in the global arena.

This chair would provide undergraduates with exposure to global business and help them to become proficient enough to transact business worldwide. We designated another half million dollars to help students acclimate themselves when hired internationally. The first trustee professor was Harry Lane, who did a phenomenal job fostering awareness of international cultures among Northeastern students. We continue to be good friends with Harry and his wife, Anne. The new Brodsky Trustee Professor is Ruth Aguilera, who is a Harvard PhD, a top researcher in her field, and an absolutely delightful woman who continues the tradition of educating students on global business and cultural differences. Darla and I continue to be involved with the International Business Program at Northeastern.

In addition to Northeastern, we also decided to help the University of Michigan. When they constructed a new building for the Ross School of Business, we donated a million dollars toward the construction of the boardroom, which now has our name on it. I also served on the Alumni Board and Board of Governors for almost twenty-five years, and still enjoy learning about the notable achievements of the Ross School of Business alumni.

As a part of my estate plan created in 1983, we conceived of a Foundation to be the beneficiary of our estates. In 1999, we funded the Brodsky Family Foundation with a small amount of seed money to make sure that the administrative provisions worked the way we intended. The Foundation is committed to preserving and protecting the environment, saving companion animals, protecting marine mammals, birds of prey, wolves, tigers, lions, cheetahs, and leopards, and to protecting against the unnecessary euthanization of domestic animals. We support various anti-poaching efforts because I despise those who needlessly slaughter any animal, either for sport or for their own ego. Irresponsible hunters are small and petty people who need to compensate for their own inadequacies and lack of self-esteem by taking an innocent life, sometimes in a canned hunt situation, where the animal has no chance of survival. Those types of hunters, and fisherman who don't catch-and-release endangered species, are not people I'll ever associate with.

We put rules in place for our Foundation, stating that an organization can only receive funds from the Foundation for ten consecutive years before they would have to take two years off, and that no one organization can receive more than 10 percent of the Foundation's annual giving. All of those rules have worked out very well administratively.

In addition to Darla and me, the board consists of our attorney, David Rosenberg; my Controller from Trammell Crow, David Jacobs; and Paul Dyer, who had been the Chairman of the Dallas Park and Recreation Department for thirty years. I got to work closely with Paul during my tenure on the Board of the Dallas Zoological Society and as Chairman of the Aquarium Committee. We have since added Peter Farren's son and my godson, Ben, to the board. We have now been operating the Foundation for over twenty years and have given away over a half million dollars to worthy causes such as the World Wildlife Fund, the International Fund for Animal Welfare, the Cousteau Society, Oceana, and several other causes.

Darla and I have become staunch environmentalists. There were a few initiatives we've become interested in since 2004 when we purchased a summer home in Fairhaven, Massachusetts, where we typically spend four months out of the year. One was the sale of undersized lobsters. It might not sound like a big deal, but it can decimate the lobster industry. We saw a grocery store selling these undersized lobsters and got them to complain to their supplier. They stopped buying undersized lobsters and notified their headquarters of the problem.

We've also used the Foundation to protect whales, turtles, and other marine mammals who are getting caught in nets discarded by fishermen. Ten percent of the debris in our oceans all over the world comes from discarded fishing gear. We're trying to create a more environmentally friendly and commercially reasonable way for fishermen to recycle their old or damaged equipment. One idea was to put transponders on the gear so it could be tracked, but that didn't sit well with the commercial fishermen. Now, we're working with the Coast Guard, the Marine Science Center at Northeastern, and contacts at Waste Management to set up receiving stations for fishermen to exchange their gear for a credit that can be used for fuel.

The Foundation is also funding part of a campaign in Iceland and Norway through the IFAW (International Fund for Animal Welfare) to stop whaling, and it has been extremely successful in getting a lot of restaurants to stop offering whale meat to tourists. We've been working locally with Oceana to get a national ban passed on finning sharks, which is a brutal process where fishermen chop off the fins of a live shark and throw it back into the water. Eventually, the shark drowns since it can't swim without its fins. However, our Senator in Florida, Marco Rubio, is supported by the shark fin industry and has become the single most significant impediment to the ban. There is no nutritional value in shark fin meat, but it's considered a delicacy and the desire for it is perpetuated by the greed of politicians and the shark fin industry.

In Africa, we've been involved in anti-poaching initiatives, and our friend Roger Snoble, who was the head of Dallas Area Rapid Transit, introduced us to David "Jonah" Western, who was the head of the Kenya Wildlife Service. Jonah had written a book called *In the Dust of Kilimanjaro* and was on a U.S. book tour in 2001 when we met him. Jonah said to let him know if we were going to Africa, and he'd help us set up the trip. Seeing Africa was a dream for Darla, so we made plans to travel to the west coast of Kenya and stay at a resort called Hemingway's to begin a three-week trip. We went to Amboseli Park where Jonah did much of his elephant research, visited the national parks, and tried scuba diving with the whale sharks. While we never actually saw any whale sharks, Darla got the opportunity to scratch the throat of a large green moray eel that was a pet of the local divemaster. We've been back to Africa three more times since.

We are now turning our attention to the Northwest Passage, where ice is melting at a rapid pace because of global warming and climate change. The high number of passenger vessels that travel from Greenland to Nome, Alaska, and into Siberia are polluting pristine waters and exposing the indigenous Inuit and Native Alaskan communities to various contaminants they've never been exposed to before. We're working on setting the cruising standards because greed has overtaken common sense in order to achieve a temporary benefit, and other people are left to clean up the mess at ten times the cost. We can avoid that by establishing parameters and setting standards that would benefit the planet.

Wildlife and animals have always been close to my heart. It goes back to the Dr. Doolittle books I read as a child and having respect for every living thing. I'll continue this effort for as long as I'm around. The Brodsky Family Foundation will be the beneficiary of my and Darla's estate, which will be sizeable and allow environmental organizations to continue doing a lot of good work. That, to me, is what determines success. It's not the money you have in the bank, but the good things you do and being able to leave some slice of the world better than it was when you found it. That can mean little things, too. Whenever we travel to a beach, we always pick up the plastic and the trash, so the beach looks a little better than when we arrived.

Despite having no children, it's important to both Darla and me to protect our environment for future generations, which is why I'm so frustrated with those who fail to recognize that rollbacks of air, water, and soil protections only increase potential health risks, mostly for those who cannot afford proper healthcare. The justification given for these rollbacks is that loosening regulations would increase employment, but that's a ruse. Greed is the root cause, and the benefits primarily accrue at the top in the form of bonuses and increased stock prices. Employment really does not change—that is driven by demand. If you argue that the cost of doing business would increase with greater environmental protections, I'd argue that sustainable production over time results in much greater efficiencies both domestically and internationally. How much will China need to spend to eliminate the pollution in its air and water, not to mention the loss of productivity from its labor force due to health problems? For the time being, labor is cheaper in China, but there will be a time when increased productivity in healthy economies and lower transportation costs will cancel out the benefits of so-called "cheap labor." Greed should not excuse unhealthy decision-making and polluters should be held accountable and be required to clean up their messes, even if it means filing bankruptcy. Those who make the decision to pollute should be personally liable for the consequences of their actions.

After retiring, my attention may have been focused on these other endeavors that are close to my heart, but I didn't completely remove myself from the real estate world. Shortly after setting up the Foundation, I became a mentor for business school students at Southern Methodist University. For more than ten years, I was assigned two or three students who have an interest in real estate, and I talk to them about business and the industry. I make myself available to answer their questions, act as a source for introductions, and help provide them with an entree into the real estate community.

I've made a lot of friends in the real estate community. We became close because we went through hell together, especially during the 1985-1995 period, but a lot of us lost touch over the years. In an attempt to reunite with my old colleagues in Dallas, I got together with Terry Gwin, Robert Grunnah, John Zouzelka, and Don Plunk to create OFORE, which stands for "Old Farts of Real Estate." The idea was to schmooze, reminisce, and tell bad stories and lies among a group of people who didn't cross paths anymore. The only rule was that you had to have spent twenty-five years working in real estate to be eligible to join. It was a social thing, and every year we threw a party at the Bent Tree Country Club, complete with an open bar and all kinds of food, and over one hundred people would attend. The club lasted twelve years and had some notable members, including Vance Miller, Craig Hall, and former Dallas Cowboy Roger Staubach, who went into real estate after his playing days.

I enjoyed my career immensely, but the water has always remained one of my first loves. When we were building *My Way*, I never would have guessed that it would end up on the list of stressors in my life that I identified in the Odyssey course, but she was becoming a burden. I was reluctant to let her go, but we had been traveling around the world and not using the boat like we used to. She required a lot of maintenance, and she wasn't worth refurbishing because I was no longer getting the same charter money that I was before Hurricane Hugo hit in 1989. It was also hard to find a good crew, so after eighteen years, it was time to sell the boat and look for a new one.

Darla and I were in Rotterdam in 2003 having dinner at a restaurant when we got the call that the contract to sell *My Way* had been accepted. At that exact moment, the Sinatra song "My Way" started playing in the background at the restaurant. The person who bought her was Terry Anderson, the priest who had been held captive in the Middle East. He renamed her *Freedom*, and the boat has remained in charter to this day.

When it was time to get a new boat, Darla didn't want a boat with sails, so in 2005 I bought a forty-three-foot trawler—a powerboat that I learned how to drive by hitting everything in sight. In 2007, I earned my one-hundred-ton Masters' Class Captain license. Darla earned her one-hundred-ton license a few years later. During the three-week course, we learned about tides, currents, and navigation. Then we bought a fifty-nine-foot Symbol powerboat five years later from a broker we had met in Seattle when we were on a cruise to Alaska. Five years after that, we built a seventy-foot Outer-Reef trawler before moving up to the Ocean Alexander 85, *Second Star*, which we have today.

Our Symbol powerboat was in Florida, and once we started cruising more, we were always driving back and forth from Texas, so in 2012, we felt that it was time to move to Fort Lauderdale. We considered other destinations and looked at San Diego, but there aren't a lot of cruising destinations from there. Other than Catalina Island, there is no place to cruise unless you want to take a thousand-mile trip down the Baja. If we kept the boat in Florida, we could go to the Caribbean and the Bahamas. Today, we take the boat out four or five times a year. Our schedule has evolved, so we'll take a long trip at the beginning of the year for eight to twelve weeks, and then two or three shorter trips, mostly to the Bahamas, and long weekends up and down the Florida coast.

We're now what people call blue water cruisers, which means that we'll go offshore at least a hundred miles. When you're offshore that far, it's easy to run into problems, and it's the Coast Guard whom you need to rely on to save your backside when you get in a bind. Out on the water, we always have the VHF radio tuned to Channel 16, the emergency channel, so we get to listen to all the calls and see the situations that the Coast Guard is responding to. They get some serious calls that involve boats sinking and catching fire. When someone is badly hurt, then they'll send in a helicopter for the rescue.

Listening to that station gave us such insight into the crucial role the Coast Guard plays for everyone who is out on the water. We started attending some of the events for The Coast Guard Foundation, which is a support organization for the U.S. Coast Guard. We were able to meet the members, or Coasties, and were really impressed by the heroic stories those young men and women had to tell. The Boston Search and Rescue team worked twelve-hour shifts, and there was nothing for them to do when they took a break, so we supplied a set of weights, weight rack, and benches, so they could relax and work out between their shifts.

The Coast Guard may be a branch of the military, but they report to Homeland Security, so it's a different structure compared to the Army, the Navy, Marines, and the Air Force. During the government shutdown in 2018, we got even more involved because the Coasties weren't getting paid at all. That's when we provided donations for gas cards and credit cards, so they could get groceries and other necessities.

When we were asked by a member of the Board of Trustees if we wanted to get even more involved, we jumped at the chance. I was first elected to the board as a trustee, and later, during their 2019 annual meeting in Houston, I was named to the Board of Directors of the Coast Guard Foundation. That means I'm currently involved in the direction of the foundation and its annual budget. We recently set up a fund called the Red Stripe Endowment to support Coast Guard scholarships, mascots and working animals, lifestyle enhancement, and a fund for the foundation Chairman and President to use as they see necessary. We do it all because supporting the Coast Guard is just something that goes along with boating. Those men and women do an incredible job and are heroes, in my personal opinion. I'm very proud to be part of that organization.

EPILOGUE

A S I APPROACH MY EIGHTIETH BIRTHDAY, I've come to realize that growing older is a full-time job. While the sunburns of my youth are turning me into a dermatological case study, I try to balance staying healthy in the face of COVID-19 with a decadent affinity for food and wine.

Today, I'm an insular person, and that's by choice. Life is too short, and I would rather spend it with Darla and my dogs, and on our boat than waste it with anyone who does not share my values or priorities. Darla has been my very best friend since we met in 1978. We've been together through health problems and financial problems. She manages me with great finesse and carefully chooses her battles, so that her direction and guidance is not obvious, though her positive impact can be felt. She makes a significant difference in my life. We share everything, and she is the best judge of character I know, which often compensates for my optimistic assessment of people.

I don't need many other people around me. I'm comfortable with myself, and I don't mind being alone. That works for me, but the dozen or so very close friends I do have, I've had for a very long time. I'm still close with my college girlfriend Ginny Fair, née Rizzo. We first met in the early 1960s, and she even attended my wedding. She's always been gracious with her concerns as we both age—she more gracefully than I. Bucky Grader from Northeastern remains a good friend. We competed in squash, racquetball, and golf. Bucky brings out my competitive spirit more than anyone else I know. Terry Gwin has remained a good friend since our first real estate deal with Ward and Stewart Hunt, and his ex-wife Susan has become a close friend who shares our passion for animals. David Jacobs, my Controller at Trammell Crow in the 1970s, is now a trustee of the family Foundation. Peggy (Burns) Hartigan remains another friend of mine who I first met over fifty years ago during our days at Dasol. Darla and I have shared many celebrations with Alec Clapperton over the years, from special birthdays to the weddings of his boys. Karen Bryan, my secretary for many years, still works with us and takes care of our Dallas financial obligations.

Peter Farren is probably my best friend, next to Darla. Our relationship may have started on a combative note as we tried to hash out the Trammell Crow Madrid deal, but it evolved over the years. He was the best man at my wedding and continues to support me with his prodigious intellect and insights. His wife, Vicky, tolerates me with good humor, and is one of the most creative people I know when it comes to culinary skills, gardening, and decorating absolutely anything. I'm godfather to their first child, Ben, and Darla is godmother to Jessica, while we both adopted the role of being godparents to Amy. As of this writing, the three Farren children have seven children among them. They've become an extended family of sorts that we have a lot of fun with, so even though Darla and I don't have any children, that doesn't mean we don't have a family.

It's been a tremendous pleasure to relive all of these experiences, but had you told me early on in my life how it would all unfold, I don't know if I would have believed any of it. Then again, I never had a vision for my future. I set out to be an astrophysicist, but I was too immature for college at seventeen and had to grow up. I didn't have a plan for how to do that. I was first shaped by those who raised me. My father was aggressive but had great common sense. My mother had joie de vivre and the ability to read people. My grandmother was tough and accepted nothing but the truth. Uncle Walter was smart and a true entrepreneur who shared his sister's love of life. I like to think that I'm a mixture of all these characteristics and traits. As I grew older, I was influenced by those whom I crossed paths with, be it the guys from the French Foreign Legion, Nicki who ran the bar in Aix, or the guys I met while in the Army. I have met and associated with all kinds of people—the good, bad, ugly, poor, rich, humble, arrogant, ignorant, aggressive, meek, competent, and the really stupid. Arguably, the worst combination is arrogance and ignorance.

Much of what I experienced came together by sheer accident, and while luck and happenstance may have opened some doors, it was my curiosity that allowed me to walk through them. I learned how to get around Paris by getting lost in almost every quadrant of the city. It took a year, but finally, it all came together. The same thing happens intellectually, and I believe that intellectual curiosity goes along with the entrepreneurial spirit. You may not realize the benefit of what you learned until a couple of years down the road, but one day it will click.

Because of my experiences with Cappy and Podmolik, I was never reluctant to ask a question or tell anyone that I didn't know something. That's a quality that has helped me throughout my life in everything I've done. Whether it's boating or economics, I don't accept anything at face value, and I don't mind challenging anyone, even the so-called experts, if I don't understand something. If you are knowledgeable about a subject, you should be able to explain it to anyone. If you can't do that, I'm going to assume that you don't know what you're talking about. I enjoy challenging those who are uninformed or pompous. If I am wrong in my opinion, I readily admit my error and am happy to have learned something new. That's why I always make sure to express my opinion in a considered way when I believe that I know what I'm talking about. And I am very opinionated. People thought I was a difficult child, and more than a few think I'm difficult today.

I was a Trustee at Northeastern University for eleven years, and whenever I raised my hand to ask questions, some of the people in the room inevitably cringed. "Oh, really? Here comes Fred again." That's happened a lot, but some of these same people invariably come up to me after the meeting and say, "I'm glad you asked that question. I wanted to ask it but didn't." I never had that problem. It's my duty to know the facts and expose any concerns to those making the decisions. It would be irresponsible of me as a leader to keep quiet and not raise questions. Leaders should be challenged and should surround themselves with smart people to compensate for any deficiencies or blind spots they might have. I enjoy being in that role, and I get that from my early mentors, Cappy—who paid such meticulous attention to detail—and Podmolik, who was always direct. That's what I've tried to do throughout my life, much to the consternation of others, for I have succeeded in antagonizing many as the politically correct mode of questioning is simply not in my nature.

I am not smart enough to lie and remember the details afterward, so I simply don't lie. If I don't know something, I ask or look it up myself. I would rather promise less and produce a greater result than overpromise and disappoint. If a price is too high, I negotiate almost everything when buying a product not made by the seller. I try to respect the workmanship when buying something actually made by the seller. If the seller is an intermediary, I negotiate like hell to get the best price. If a workman offers to reduce his price too much, I do not use him, as I will not be happy with the result. If buying a commodity, like a car, I want the best price since service is not performed by the salesman. I want to be around happy people who take pride in their work and are fair and reasonable when problems or the unforeseen arise. I hold people to their word, the spirit of their word, and any agreements we might have. If a deal turns out to be seriously unfair, or if I have offered more for a service or product than warranted, I live with my mistakes and do not blame others for my problems. I've learned to appreciate that it's better to be who you are in life, and to have consistent standards when it comes to the character, honesty, and integrity of relationships you choose. However, I also have a long memory. When a "friend" ran into financial problems while building his new boat in England, I loaned him money to finish construction. He didn't pay me back. After I froze his bank account, he wrote a check that bounced. I still hold a grudge after that experience and always will when someone takes advantage of my good intentions.

I've failed often. I experienced plenty of ups and downs, successes and failures, but I'm not any different than any other entrepreneur. We all go through something similar. It's how you handle those challenges that is important—that's what makes us who we are. Some people can't handle the downs, whether they're physical, mental, monetary, or health related. It's easy for people to dwell on problems, stop their lives completely, and refuse to accept the consequences of whatever they are doing. Continuing to make this same mistake will result in failure. That's not a productive way to go through life. Others, to their credit, can overcome those problems and learn from them. I like to think that

I've benefited from the latter: it's not just what you do, but how you do it that matters.

For me, life is about getting out there, seeking opportunities, and challenging yourself. You want excitement and stimulation. You want to feel good and be healthy. You want to contribute something to the world and enjoy yourself while doing it. Darla and I have been fortunate enough to visit a Viet Cong general in his home, a Masai chief in his mud hut, Inuit villages in Nunavut, Canada, a United States Ambassador at her residence in Vienna, and various families on every continent. In 2006, we were on a cruise that took us from Buenos Aires and around the tip of South America to Lima, Peru. We were in a remote area, and it was cold as hell, but one of the things we were able to do was get on a Russian-made helicopter and fly over the glaciers to a whale preservation research center. There, we put on survival suits and boarded a Zodiac boat with a group of researchers to check in on the health of two massive humpback whales that stayed with us for over one hour only feet away from the boat.

Experiences like that are the spice of life and provide the type of satisfaction that you can't get from sitting at home and watching TV or reading a book. It's just something you have to go out and experience for yourself. Often, these experiences aren't easy and force you to get out of your comfort zone, but they are supposed to be difficult. The worst thing I've ever heard someone say is "I can't do that," when in fact, they're talking about something they really want to do. I think that attitude, in most cases, is shortsighted. Instead, let's figure out another way to get it done. It's that attitude that has helped me experience the greatest pleasures in life. I'm not special in that regard—anybody can do that and be successful! If you work really hard, have the right priorities, remain persistent, and if you aren't afraid to take some chances in order to get what you want, you're going to grow, expand your horizons, and live a stimulating and satisfying life, even without any master plan.

Hopefully, my life is far from being over. I'm approaching my eightieth birthday, and still have no definitive plan but there remains so much to see, enjoy, and share with Darla. We're looking forward to a three-month trip on Second Star to the Bahamas, Dominican Republic, Columbia (for the first time), Cayman, Belize, and Mexico early in 2021. We also want to visit the small islands just north of Antarctica and south of New Zealand. Our mantra continues to be: "Let's do as much as we can for as long as we can!"

ENJOY AND BE SAFE